THE SOUND OF GOD

A Convergence of Sound, Science & Scripture

Marcia Alverson
Remnant Rising Co. Publishing

COPYRIGHT INFORMATION

This publication is intended for educational and inspirational purposes only. It is not intended to provide scientific, medical, legal, or professional advice. The views expressed in this book are those of the author and are presented as a personal exploration of the relationship between faith, sound, and the natural world.

While this work draws thoughtful parallels between observable patterns in creation and the spiritual truths described in Scripture, it does not claim to offer measurable or empirical proof of the voice of God. Rather, it invites readers into a deeper consideration of the harmony between the physical and spiritual realms as understood through faith.

This book was created with the assistance of modern digital tools for editing and design; however, the ideas, structure, and authorship with full editing are the original work of the author.

Published by Remnant Rising Co.
Cover design by Marcia Alverson
Author photo by Marcia Alverson

ISBN: 979-8-9954357-0-9

First Edition

This book is dedicated to my *family*.
My husband, my *forever* love, Braeden.
Our amazing kids, Josiah and Abigail.
May you be *firmly rooted* in Love,
faithful in your pursuit of Truth,
and *fearless* to roam where He leads,
Knowing His voice will always *find* you
and lead you Home.
I love you always.

THE SOUND OF GOD

PREFACE

A Safe Place for Honest Faith

This book was not written to convince you.
It was written to meet you.

If you come to these pages skeptical, cautious, wounded, curious, or quietly unconvinced, you are not out of place here. In many ways, you are exactly who this book was written for. The God revealed in Scripture has never been threatened by honest questions, and faith has never required the suspension of thought. What it requires is openness—an openness to encounter rather than control, to relationship rather than reduction.

Much of what passes for faith today is inherited, syndicated, or performed. Many of us learned how to speak about God long before we learned how to listen for Him. Over time, this creates a quiet dissonance: the language remains, but the resonance fades. We repeat truths we no longer feel connected to and defend beliefs we were never invited to examine.

This book does not ask you to abandon Scripture, reason, or discernment. It asks something more difficult—that you allow them to work together rather than compete. Science is not presented here as a replacement for faith, nor as a courtroom where God must be proven. It is treated as what it is: a witness. A testimony of order, coherence, and design that quietly points beyond itself.

Scripture remains the anchor—not as a weapon to silence questions, but as a living voice meant to be heard, received, and embodied.

If you have ever sensed that God has been reduced by the systems meant to represent Him, grown weary of answers that feel rehearsed rather than revealed, or suspected that faith must be more than agreement with ideas—this is your invitation. You do not need to arrive with certainty. You only need to arrive willing.

This is a space where questions are not punished, doubt is not shamed, and reverence is not confused with fear. The posture here is not defensive but attentive. The aim is not to standardize belief, but to retune perception—to clear the static so that what remains is the Sound of God as He truly is.

Why I Wrote This the Way I Did

I am a Christ follower.

I am also skeptical of the ways God has been filtered, managed, and marketed through human systems. That tension is not a contradiction—it is part of my faith journey.

Humanity often tries sincerely to represent God. Yet many structures built to help us understand Him have unintentionally made it harder to know Him. Somewhere along the path, encounter was replaced with explanation, reverence with performance, and relationship with regulation.

This book is not an attempt to dismantle faith.
It is an attempt to clear space for it.

I write not as someone who has arrived, but as someone who has wrestled—who has loved the church, been disappointed by it, learned from it, and sometimes stepped back in order to hear God more clearly. I have questioned not because I wanted distance, but because I wanted honesty.

Throughout these pages you will notice a refusal to overexplain God. That is not vagueness—it is reverence. God is not meant to be fully understood, only known. Scripture reminds us that we see truly, but not completely. Faith therefore grows not through intellectual mastery but through relational trust.

Science is treated with similar humility. It observes what exists; it does not define the Source of existence. Where it reveals order and pattern, it quietly testifies to design. Where it reaches its limits, it stops.

If you are reading this while carrying disappointment, fatigue, or doubt, hear this clearly: God is not offended by your honesty. He does not require you to defend Him, perform for Him, or pretend certainty you do not possess. What He desires is connection.

My hope is that these pages offer a place to lay down borrowed language and rediscover your own voice with God—to move from secondhand faith to lived encounter.

If you allow it, this journey will not simply give you new ideas. It will retune your posture. And from that alignment, faith will stop feeling like something you must hold together and begin feeling like something that holds you.

Why Science and Sound Matter

Observing sound in motion through the study of **cymatics** became the unexpected discovery that led me to write this book. My first encounter with cymatics awakened something deep within me. As I began exploring the nature of sound and vibration, familiar Scriptures I had known for years began to surface again—but in a completely new light.

Watching patterns emerge from sound felt like witnessing a conversation between the unseen and the visible, a reminder that the Word of God is not merely spoken into the world but actively sustaining it. In that moment something shifted inside me. The Scriptures I had read so many times no longer felt like declarations on a page, grasped only through the invisible marker of faith. They felt alive—tangible, present, almost within reach. Faith itself was becoming substance to me. It was as though I was hearing the Word of God again, yet somehow for the very first time.

A new dimension of understanding opened—a deeper awareness of God and of my place within His creation. I was no longer trying to impress a distant deity with my behavior. I was learning to hear His voice and respond as I was designed to.

In that response I found alignment—spirit, soul, and body.

Standing before a room of Bible students in 2017, sharing some of these principles, I said aloud, "One day I will write a book about this." That spontaneous moment became the seed—and eventually the structure—of the book you are about to read.

Yet the journey of writing it has felt much like the magi following the North Star toward Bethlehem. I did not know exactly where the path would lead, but I sensed the unmistakable invitation to follow. And in following His voice, I discovered something profound: the voice calling me forward was the very same voice unmistakably holding the universe together.

I heard clearly from the Lord: "I need you to write this because you are a worshiper."

That was not a compliment. It was an assignment.

This would not be a book replacing Scripture with science or spirituality with spectacle. It would be a book about alignment—staying tethered to the Source while exploring the echoes of His design.

When people hear words like frequency and resonance, they often drift in one of two directions: suspicion or fascination. Some chase power without intimacy. Others pursue revelation without reverence. But worship keeps the heart anchored. If there is a central burden in these pages, it is this:

Do not chase the phenomenon and miss the Person.

We are living in an age of endless content—AI, social media, and constant streams of information. It has never been easier to repeat someone else's revelation while neglecting personal communion with God.

This book is meant to gently call us back to the one thing. Where your attention goes, your worship goes. And worship, rightly aimed, restores clarity. My prayer is that these chapters invite you into something simple but life-changing: learning to hear God for yourself.

The Kingdom does not thrive on borrowed oil. It flourishes when each heart becomes personally connected to the living Voice—when faith is awakened through communion.

And the good news is this: it is not difficult.

You were designed for it. You were created to recognize Him.
You were formed to resonate with Him.

You were made to hear the Sound of God.

INTRODUCTION

This book is a journey through a sequence I did not engineer—I received it as a blueprint.

Before I knew how the pieces would fit, the Lord impressed the chapter titles upon me like coordinates: **Alpha, Architect, Adam, Archetype, Awakening, Adoration, Alignment, Assignment and Axiom.**

Each one is a doorway. Each one is a threshold. Together they trace a path that moves the soul from information to revelation, from familiarity to reverence, from passive belief to living recognition.

To experience this book, follow the coordinates.

Everything in the universe vibrates.

Sound is vibration moving through a medium, expressed as waves with measurable frequency. These waves do not merely travel—they organize. Through resonance, one vibrating system can influence another, causing it to move, change, or align.

Cymatics makes this invisible reality visible, revealing how sound can form matter into ordered patterns. Sound does not create chaos—it creates structure.

If we are created in the image of a God who spoke creation into existence, then perhaps our ability to speak, resonate, and bring order through sound reflects something deeper about how the world itself began.

With that possibility in mind, the journey begins.

Alpha

Alpha calls us back to first things—the beginning beneath all beginnings—where the Word is not a religious ornament but the originating reality. Here the reader is invited to consider that creation itself bears the signature of speech: order, pattern, rhythm, resonance. Not as a gimmick of science, but as a whisper of Scripture—that God does not merely make; He utters, and what He utters becomes.

Architect

Architect opens the blueprint. If God builds, what does He see as He forms? What does He call good, and why does goodness have shape, structure, and intention? In this portion of the journey we explore the intelligence behind creation—an artistry that is not chaotic or impulsive, yet deeply personal. The question begins to shift from *"Can I define God?"* to *"Can I trust the One who designed me to hear Him?"*

Adam

Then comes Adam—not as a distant story but as a mirror. If humanity was formed in His image, could it mean we were designed to resonate with Him? That our inner life carries the capacity to receive, respond, and harmonize with the Creator? Here faith begins to look less like climbing toward God and more like awakening to a signal that has been present all along—Christ calling, breath filling lungs, light entering places we once kept closed.

Archetype

Archetype reveals recurring patterns—spiritual shapes that appear again and again because God is consistent. Just as melodies repeat within a song, themes return in the life of a believer: invitation, wilderness, surrender, encounter, commission. These are not random emotional cycles; they are pathways of formation. And as the pattern becomes visible, so does the Voice behind it.

Awakening

Awakening is the moment the signal becomes personal—not louder, but clearer. It is the shift from knowing about God to realizing you are being addressed by Him. Something in you stirs—not as emotional hype, but as recognition, like hearing your name spoken in a crowded room. Faith begins to feel less like collecting answers and more like receiving Presence.

Adoration

Adoration moves the journey from thought to posture. Worship is not merely music or mood; it is orientation. It is the heart turning toward the Source—reverence without distance, intimacy without contempt. Here God is no longer treated as a concept to manage, but as the Holy One to behold. Familiarity loosens its grip, and wonder returns.

Alignment

Alignment is where the signal reshapes the soul. Stillness is not emptiness—it is tuning. It is the quiet courage to let God be God—unreduced, undomesticated—and to allow ourselves to be adjusted by His nearness. In a world trained to hurry and perform, this becomes a different kind of strength: the strength to listen long enough to remember what we were made for.

Assignment

Assignment carries awakening outward. If God is speaking, it is not only to comfort—it is to commission. The Sound of God does not end in a private moment; it bears fruit in a lived response. When the signal grows clear, obedience becomes possible, and the reader begins to sense something deeper stirring: *I am not here by accident. I am here for partnership.*

Axiom

The final chapter gathers the steady truths beneath all creation—the ways of God that do not fluctuate with culture or fear. These are not cold laws but stabilizing realities. They anchor faith in something stronger than emotion and teach us to live from the eternal rather than the urgent.

How to best read this book:

You are not entering a lecture; you are entering a listening room.

You may have picked up this book because you thought you were hungry to learn more about God, science, or new ways of understanding the world. But perhaps what your spirit is truly craving is not more information—it is ***holy repetition, restored rhythm***, and a way of processing reality through the lens you were always meant to carry.

Read slowly. Pause when something stirs.

Create the space your spirit longs for so that you can truly experience the Sound of God with all the noise around you. Let silence and "selah" become part of the journey. You do not have to arrive certain, polished, or spiritually impressive. Bring the honest version of yourself—the questions you carry quietly, the places faith has felt thin, the longing you cannot quite explain.

If God is truly living and present, then He is not offended by your hunger. He may be the One who placed it there. This is the threshold where familiarity loosens its grip and reverence returns. Alpha is not merely the beginning of time. It is the beginning of hearing.

Enter Alpha.

ALPHA

In the Beginning Was the Word — Sound as the First Act of Creation

Before time was measured—before form emerged, before motion began—Scripture opens on a scene that feels almost impossible to describe without reverence.

"In the beginning, God created the heavens and the earth." — Genesis 1:1

Darkness rests upon the face of the deep.

The world is not yet organized into what we recognize as life, and yet the silence is not empty. It is attentive. Expectant. Holy.

"The Spirit of God was hovering over the waters" (Genesis 1:2).

That single line carries more weight than we often realize. Hovering suggests presence without intrusion—nearness without force. Like an artist lingering over a blank canvas, not because vision is lacking, but because the first stroke matters.

Then something happens that changes everything.

God speaks.

"And God said, 'Let there be light,' and there was light." - Genesis 1:3

Not a wave of the hand.
Not an explosion.
But a voice. God's voice.

A word released into the deep. Suddenly the beginning does not feel like a distant theological concept. It feels intimate. Immediate. Alive.

When God speaks—darkness yields.

For most of my life, I have read Genesis with an emphasis on *what* God created: light, sky, land, seas, living creatures, humanity. I believed it all. I taught it. I admired it. But I rarely considered *how* He created. This time, I felt compelled to read it again. My filter had shifted. It was no longer just a story to see the details- but the very blueprints of God's handiwork.

I ran across a video about cymatics, which is the study of the visualization of sound and vibration. Because we cannot see airwaves vibrate, cymatics shows how sound interacts with physical matter by revealing the patterns vibration creates.

It wasn't merely interesting; it was arresting. Tone after tone, frequency after frequency, patterns began to appear—shapes emerging in response to what could not be seen. A change in frequency and the form reorganized. The unseen made itself known by the order it produced. I felt my heart leap the way it does when something ancient becomes immediate—when knowledge stops being information and starts becoming recognition.

It wasn't that cymatics "proved" Scripture. That isn't the point. Something in me simply recognized a possibility I had not fully considered: the invisible is not imaginary. The unseen can be real, measurable, and consequential. Sound travels through air as pressure waves, carrying energy, information, and—when met with a receptive system—meaning.

We cannot see a note, but we can feel it move through us. We can watch it shape a room, calm a child, stir grief, awaken courage. We cannot hold sound in our hands, yet it can rearrange the inside of us in seconds. As a musician, I have lived that truth. And I began to wonder: what if Scripture has been speaking this language all along?

I went back to Genesis and read it again, and it was as if a fresh lens had been placed over the text. "And God said…" This is how God created. With His voice. I was astonished—not because the words were new, but because I was new in the way I was hearing them. A quiet, steady impression rose in my spirit: ***Now you see how I move.***

It reminded me of the first time I ever put on eyeglasses at the tender age of ten. I didn't realize my vision needed help so badly. I remember the shock of detail—leaves on trees I had never truly *seen* before. Not because the leaves weren't there, but because my vision had been limited. That is what it felt like to read "And God said…" again. **The Word didn't change. My perception did**. And once I saw it, I couldn't unsee it.

Maybe this is part of what it means to "know" God. We can know a great deal *about* Him and never truly see His ways. Like someone who can recite facts about a public figure but has never sat with them, never listened closely enough to learn their tone, their pauses, their compassion—the *personhood* behind the information. Scripture is holy. The stories matter. The doctrines matter. But what if the heartbeat beneath the text is not merely instruction—it is a rhythm to respond to? God's voice hidden in plain sight, reaching deeper than our familiarity, calling for encounter.

And something happens when encounter becomes possible: the Bible stops being a distant record and becomes a living interface. Not a flat page, but a doorway. The Word begins to feel embodied—not because we are inventing meaning, but because we are finally perceiving what was there all along. The God of the Word is living and breathing, and He does not merely want to be studied; He longs to be known.

As Genesis unfolds, we watch the heavens stretch wide, waters separate, land emerge, life fill its appointed place. Each phrase carries more than sound; it carries intention. And eventually humanity enters the harmony—formed with care, bearing His image, animated by His breath (Genesis 2:7). We are not accidental. We are not afterthought. We are crafted, and then—somehow—God shares something of His own life with us.

So here is a question worth holding with reverence: why does it matter that creation begins with God speaking? Perhaps because His voice is not merely symbolic. Perhaps it is central. The Word is not an accessory to creation; it appears to be the means through which form and life emerge at all. If creation begins with utterance, then faith may be less about blind belief and more about resonance—about learning to respond to the One who is already speaking beneath the surface of everything.

God as Spirit, Not Form — Reframing How We Perceive Divine Presence

It is tempting to reduce God to what we can picture—to prefer Him familiar, manageable, human-shaped, mind-sized, emotion-sized. But Scripture quietly refuses that narrowing: "God is spirit" (John 4:24). That line alone disrupts so many of our assumptions. Spirit is not less real; it is differently real. Invisible does not mean absent. Unseen does not mean unreal.

We live with invisible realities constantly. Gravity cannot be seen, yet it orders our entire physical experience. Electricity is invisible, yet it powers our homes and carries our voices across continents. Radio waves fill the air, though we remain unaware until a receiver is tuned to them. (Electromagnetic waves; signal; reception) The unseen can be foundational. The question is not whether it exists; the question is whether we are positioned to perceive it.

A phrase often attributed to Nikola Tesla says, *"If you want to find the secrets of the universe, think in terms of energy, frequency, and vibration."* Whether or not he said it exactly that way, the idea resonates with what both science and Scripture repeatedly suggest: reality is not only matter—it is movement.

Atoms are not quiet little marbles; they are active, dynamic systems. The physical world is charged with motion and pattern.

And then Scripture speaks with a strange, shimmering familiarity: "By the word of the LORD the Heavens were made, and by the breath of His mouth all their host." (Psalm 33:6) Creation described not as collision, but as utterance. Breath released. Word spoken.

What if these aren't merely poetic metaphors? What if the language of "word" and "breath" hints at a reality where sound, vibration, and resonance are not add—Ons—but foundational features of how God chose to communicate Himself into creation? Not because God is reducible to physics, but because physics may be one of the many languages through which His order is displayed.

To consider God in terms of "frequency" is not to shrink Him. It is to let wonder expand. Frequency, in scientific terms, is measured repetition—cycles per second, often measured in Hertz (Hz). (Frequency; Hz) It describes rhythm. Consistency. A signature. And perhaps that's one way to frame what Scripture keeps revealing: God's presence is not confined to form. He is not limited to what we can diagram. **He is living, moving, sustaining—present in ways that can be experienced even when they cannot be grasped.**

Before Matter: Vibration — What Creation Echoes

When you look outward into the universe, patterns emerge that feel almost musical in their order. Galaxies spiral with graceful consistency. Stars ignite, blaze, fade, and give way to others. The cosmos expands, steady and mysterious. Not frantic. Not random. It carries the feel of motion sustained rather than abandoned—like a voice that has not stopped speaking but continues to hold what it has called into being.

Closer to home, planets trace paths with remarkable precision. Earth turns, tilts, cycles through seasons in rhythms so dependable life depends on them. Tides respond to the moon with faithful cadence. Within our own bodies, rhythm persists—Hearts beating, lungs filling and releasing, nervous systems firing in patterns that keep us alive. These are not just mechanisms; they are consistent movements that feel like signatures pressed into the fabric of reality.

Science describes resonance as the phenomenon where a system responds strongly to certain frequencies—when the input "matches" the natural tendencies of the system, amplification occurs. (Resonance) In music, a string will vibrate sympathetically when another note of the same frequency is played nearby. In life, we sense resonance emotionally and spiritually, too—the way a truth can land in us with an unmistakable *yes*, even before we can explain it.

What if creation itself is filled with that kind of responsiveness? What if the rhythms are not merely mechanical, but receptive — echoes of a sustaining cadence? If God speaks, perhaps creation listens. Perhaps what we call "order" is not merely structure, but *response.*

Eternity Enters Time — How the Alpha Still Speaks

There is a haunting tenderness in the biblical idea that breath is life. "Then the LORD God formed the man of dust from the ground and breathed into his nostrils the breath of life" (Genesis 2:7). Breath is intimate. It is near. It is shared. And Scripture suggests the breath that initiates does not withdraw once the moment passes. The voice that once spoke light into darkness does not appear confined to the past.

"Behold, I am making all things new." (Revelation 21:5)

That isn't merely a future promise; it is a revelation of God's nature. He is a God who speaks again. Who renews. Who restores. Who reintroduces light into darkness—not only in the cosmos, but in the human soul.

He speaks through prophets. He speaks through poetry. He speaks through the Living Word who walked among us (John 1:14). And yes—He speaks through Scripture. But perhaps He also speaks through creation's quiet order, through the strange, holy tug in your spirit when you are near truth, through the whisper that comes when you finally stop striving long enough to listen.

Faith, then, is not an escape from reality. It may be a deeper kind of contact with reality—the unseen layer that shapes what is seen. "Now faith is the assurance of things hoped for, the conviction of things not seen." (Hebrews 11:1) The world often frames faith as imagination or wishful thinking. But Scripture calls it substance. Evidence. Not because we can control God, but because we can encounter Him.

And that encounter often works like reception. Like tuning. Not because God is fickle, but because our alignment shifts. When we drift, distortion follows. Confusion replaces clarity. It may not be that the signal failed—only that we have lost resonance. The answer may not be striving harder, but listening differently.

Before Seeing — Faith as the First Sense Awakened

Truth is not shaped by our perception of it. It does not bend with culture, opinion, or mood. God is who He is—unchanging, whole, eternal—whether we can comprehend Him or not (Exodus 3:14). And yet, Scripture is equally clear about something tender: God reveals Himself in ways we are able to behold.

We come to Him carrying different stories, wounds, assumptions, and lenses. Our understanding is partial. Our awareness incomplete. And still—God is persistent. He seeks. He calls. He draws near. He does not change His nature to accommodate error, but He does adjust the nearness of His revelation to cultivate resonance. Like a signal drawing a receiver into clarity, He pulls us toward Himself until we are able to receive what has always been true.

Faith, then, is not the creation of truth—it is awakening to truth. Not because truth evolves, but because we do. Our capacity deepens. Our humility grows. Our surrender opens space. And as that happens, the signal becomes clearer—not necessarily louder, but more recognizable. What was once faint becomes familiar. What was once mysterious becomes intimate.

Perhaps this is why Scripture so often honors hearing before seeing: "So faith comes from hearing, and hearing through the word of Christ." (Romans 10:17) Before we can explain, we can receive. Before we can map it, we can respond. **Faith may be the first sense awakened—not because we understand fully, but because our spirit recognizes what our mind cannot yet grasp.**

And this is where the invitation becomes personal.

Perhaps what was meant by "be still" was not mere relaxation, but retuning—turning down the static so the signal can be recognized again (Psalm 46:10).

One very specific encounter I had with the Lord took place after a worship time our band was leading at a camp in Oregon. The glory of the Lord felt tangible in the room—weighty, unhurried, and holy. As the service ended, people gradually began to stand and leave, as they should, carrying their own lives back into motion. But I remained bowed - something in me couldn't rush what felt sacred. I remember the weight of His presence like a mantle resting on the atmosphere.

As I started to disengage—simply because others were leaving—I sensed the still, small voice of God calling me to linger longer. *Just wait here.* So I did.

One of the ways God often speaks to me is through visions—images that rise in the "mind's eye," like a living dream while awake. In that moment, my spiritual sight opened to a bright light in the distance. It was brilliant—so bright it felt like looking into the sun—yet it carried no harshness, only holiness. I couldn't stop gazing at it. I didn't "do" anything with it. I didn't really analyze it – just observed it. The only appropriate response was to give my full attention.

The waiting lasted a long time—maybe thirty minutes. There was no dramatic message, no unfolding storyline—only that light, and the steady call to remain. Then suddenly the bright light moved close, and, in an instant, it flipped—becoming a mirror. And the mirror was beholding *me*. All I could see in myself was that same bright light.

I understood it without words: in the moments we wait on Him, we become like Him. Not by striving. Not by performing. But by beholding. By receiving. By allowing the presence of God to saturate and recalibrate. This posture was enough to signal His reflection in me and through me.

Stillness became my posture.
Beholding became my obedience.
Retuning and recalibration became my transformation.
Reflection became the outcome.

The weight of that encounter has stayed with me through my entire life. I will never forget it, because it taught me something my mind cannot manufacture — **transformation can only happen when we stop trying to control the moment and instead surrender to it.** When we pause long enough for the signal to become unmistakable, He does his transformative work in us. It's where we can begin to grasp the Scripture, "Not by might, nor by power, but by My Spirit, says the Lord." (Zechariah 4:6)

From Observation to Communion

In moments like that, I can see the beauty of God's design. It's fascinating to me the way the smallest building blocks of creation seem designed for response. In the quantum world, a system can be described as holding a range of possible outcomes—until it is *measured*, until it is brought into a genuine interaction that registers information. And then what was held in possibility becomes expressed as something definite. That doesn't mean "human eyes animate atoms," the way pop science sometimes says it. It means reality at that level is profoundly *interactive.* Measurement is an encounter—an exchange—an event that changes what can be meaningfully seen. This is why physicists talk about the measurement problem, and why decoherence matters: interaction with the environment suppresses interference effects and helps explain why the world appears stable and classical at our scale.

And when I sit with that—carefully, humbly—I don't feel like it diminishes God. It does the opposite. It makes me marvel at a Creator who did not craft a universe of inert, dead things, but a universe with responsiveness woven into its bones. A world where relationship is not an afterthought, but a signature. Where the unseen is not fantasy, but foundational. Even the famous double—slit story carries this strange echo: when "which—path" information is obtained, the interference pattern disappears; when the path remains unregistered, the pattern emerges. It's as though creation keeps whispering, in its own non—human language: *encounter matters.*

And then I feel the parallel rise in me—not as a forced comparison, but as a gentle line of wonder connecting physics to theology. If God made a world that reveals itself through encounter, could it be that we, made in His image, were designed the same way? "So God created man in his own image" (Genesis 1:27).

We aren't merely thinkers; we are beholders. We are receivers. We are relational beings whose deepest clarity does not come from collecting information, but from being met—seen, known, loved, called. Scripture doesn't describe God as an abstract concept to master. It describes Him as a Presence. A voice. A face. A glory.

And it does something astonishing: it tells us we are both invited to behold—and already being beheld. "O LORD, you have searched me and known me" (Psalm 139:1). "No creature is hidden from his sight" (Hebrews 4:13). That is not meant to crush the heart; it is meant to anchor it. The ache in us is not proof of emptiness—it may be evidence of design.

Because what are we longing to behold, really? Not merely outcomes. Not merely comfort. Not merely the feeling of being "okay." Beneath all those surface desires is a deeper hunger: to behold the One we came from—to look upon what is wholly true, wholly good, wholly alive, and to be looked upon in return without shame. "One thing have I asked of the LORD… to gaze upon the beauty of the LORD" (Psalm 27:4).

And then comes the holy mystery: beholding is not only seeing—it is becoming. "And we all, with unveiled face, beholding the glory of the Lord, are being transformed…" (2 Corinthians 3:18). That is what your Oregon moment carried in it. You weren't striving to change. You were simply willing to stay. To listen. To behold. And the mirror revealed what Scripture has been saying all along: when you behold Him, you begin to reflect Him.

So perhaps the "motion" we are searching for in life—purpose, clarity, courage, love—is not something we manufacture by willpower. Perhaps it flows in and out like breath, born from communion. "Be still and know that I am God" (Psalm 46:10) isn't a command to relax as much as it is an invitation to retune—to let the static fall quiet enough that the signal of His nearness becomes recognizable again.

And maybe this is why faith so often begins with hearing: "Faith comes from hearing, and hearing through the word of Christ" (Romans 10:17). We listen before we explain. We receive before we defend. We behold before we can fully define. Life moves again when we return to the gaze—when we allow ourselves to be beheld by Love, and we respond by beholding the One who has been there all along.

An Invitation Into the Journey

This book is written from a simple curiosity: that every person may carry an innate capacity to perceive God. His nature is good (Psalm 34:8). His intent toward creation—including you—is good. He formed all things with care, and within those things is evidence of order, beauty, and design (Psalm 19:1). Whether one chooses to believe in God or engage with Him as Deity is deeply personal. But our ability to perceive Him does not define His existence. Many realities shape our lives without ever being seen.

So I invite you—wherever you find yourself—to approach these pages with openness. Take your time. Let the ideas settle beyond the intellect. Let them interface with your whole being: mind, body, soul, and spirit (1 Thessalonians 5:23). If God's Word is living and active (Hebrews 4:12), then it is not merely meant to inform you; it is meant to *meet* you. To do something in you. To awaken recognition. To recalibrate what has drifted. To restore resonance.

You do not have to rush toward conclusions. You are allowed to wonder. You are allowed to sit at the threshold and let awe do its slow work. You are allowed to return to familiar Scriptures and read them as if you're seeing leaves on trees for the first time—because sometimes that is exactly what God is giving: a new lens, not a new Bible.

And as a musician, I can't escape this conviction: sound has always carried a kind of holy familiarity for me. It moves invisibly yet powerfully. It can comfort, convict, heal, call, and gather. And when I began to notice how Scripture repeatedly frames God as One who speaks—One whose breath creates, whose Word forms, whose voice calls—something in me recognized a harmony I had not known how to name.

Perhaps Scripture and creation are not competing voices, but layered witnesses. Perhaps the eternal Word still resonates through the very vibrations that hold creation together—not as a gimmick, not as a novelty, but as a quiet signature: God is present. God is speaking. God is not far.

The most important realization is this: the universe did not begin with noise—it began with a voice. Before matter formed, before stars burned, before life breathed, a Word was spoken into the deep. And that Word did not produce chaos; it produced order. Light separated from darkness. Waters gathered. Life emerged.

The patterns we observe today may not simply be the mechanics of nature, but the echoes of that first utterance still sustaining creation. If sound became structure, then creation was never accidental. It was intentional. And where there is intention, there is a mind behind it—a Designer who did not merely speak the universe into existence but formed it with purpose. To understand the Sound of God more fully, we must now look beyond the moment of creation and consider the One behind the voice.

Enter the Architect.

ARCHITECT

Cornerstone

The opening lines of Scripture may be more than a statement of creation; they may be our first glimpse of the Architect behind it. Scripture does not show Him improvising. It shows Him ordering. "In the beginning" arrives with calm authority, like a Builder stepping onto a site already held in His mind. The opening line is not only about beginnings; it is about intention. It reveals a God who sees the end while He stands at the start. "Declaring the end from the beginning" is how Isaiah describes Him (Isaiah 46:10), and that is an Architect's gift: to hold a finished vision while the ground is still bare.

And what does an Architect do first? He establishes foundations. He sets measurements. He marks boundaries that will protect life later. Job hints at this hidden scene when God asks, "Where were you when I laid the foundation of the earth… Who determined its measurements… or who stretched the line upon it?" (Job 38:4–5). The language is almost intimate—tape lines and cornerstones, structure and proportion. What if creation begins with God's quiet delight in coherence? Not because He needs a world to prove His strength, but because order is the language love uses when it prepares a home.

Could it be that Scripture opens the way it does because God is less interested in winning an argument than in awakening recognition? "In the beginning, God created the Heavens and the earth" (Genesis 1:1). No warm-up. No footnotes. No apology. Just a sentence that lands like a cornerstone—quiet, weighty, immovable. Before Scripture explains anything, it places Someone at the center.

What if we've missed how relational that first line actually is? It reads like a declaration, yes—but could it also be an invitation? Before mechanisms are revealed, before processes are named, before matter is described, we are offered a singular assertion: God is origin. Not merely as an idea to be evaluated, but as a reality to be encountered. Maybe the beginning of faith was never meant to feel distant. Perhaps God was never meant to be approached first as a doctrine to defend, a mystery to solve, or a concept to analyze, but as a Presence to be perceived—near enough to be known.

The Pulse of "And God Said"

"And God said…" returns like a **Heartbeat,** but perhaps it is also the sound of craftsmanship. Because architecture is never merely drawing; it is speech made visible—an idea becoming structure, a word becoming form. And if the world is framed by God's Word, then creation is not random material shaped by chance, but matter responding to intention. "By faith we understand that the universe was created by the word of God" (Hebrews 11:3). Not assembled by exertion alone but *called*—as though the Architect's voice carries both design and permission: you may exist, you may hold, you may bear life.

This makes the phrase "And God said" feel less like a narrative device and more like a revelation of how God works. He is not frantic. He is not noisy. He doesn't force the world into being by strain. He speaks—and reality aligns. Divine speech is the original blueprint, and all of creation is a faithful translation. The heavens do not argue with His command; they cooperate. The seas do not negotiate their borders; they receive them. Perhaps this is why God's Word still has such authority in a human soul. Something in us remembers being made by Voice. Something in us still responds when the Architect speaks.

And what if the refrain that follows is not just literary rhythm, but theological revelation? "And God said…" (Genesis 1:3). Over and over, like a pulse running through the veins of the text. Could it be that Genesis is quietly teaching us that creation itself is born from communication? That the world is not merely assembled, but addressed? If that is true, then God's voice is not simply informative; it is formative. His speech doesn't merely describe reality—it creates it.

To speak is to vibrate. To utter is to initiate movement. Every word we say rides on waves: breath turned into sound, sound traveling through air, air carrying signal. Even our simplest conversation is held together by physics we rarely acknowledge. And if that's true at the human level, then what might it mean to consider a God whose voice is not metaphor, but power? What if divine speech isn't just language the way we use it, but the very act of shaping being—frequency with intention, resonance with purpose?

Knowing About God, or Knowing God

Maybe this is why faith can feel complicated when we approach it primarily as information. Most of us were taught about God. Fewer of us were taught how to encounter Him. And fewer still were invited to consider that our difficulty with faith might not be God's absence, but our awareness. What if an entire dimension of relationship has always existed, quietly surrounding us—waiting not for effort, but for attention? What if God is closer than we've dared to assume, and the ache we call "distance" is really a lack of attunement?

When I began writing this book, I expected an exercise in explaining—an attempt to make ancient words feel modern, to connect spiritual language with scientific images, to build bridges between two worlds that often speak past each other. But perhaps the most surprising thing was that the writing didn't dismantle my faith; it deepened it. I felt as though I was drawing closer to God as I meditated on His Word and could see how I fit in His overall plan for all of creation. It was both humbling and comforting. I was being repositioned to be able to hear Him clearer than I had before.

It felt less like learning something new and more like discovering a room I had lived beside for years without realizing the door was open. Scripture did not lose meaning. It unfolded. Passages I had read for a long time began to carry a different kind of clarity, as though they had been waiting for a posture of presence rather than a posture of debate.

Revelation from God does not originate from intellectual understanding; it arrives as a *knowing.* As if the Truth that was dormant inside of you has now been awakened. You can feel this shift in your entire being.

Could it be that we often mistake "knowing God" for "knowing about God"? One fills the mind with facts, the other fills the heart with presence. If presence is the point, then faith begins to feel less like mental assent and more like embodied awareness—something lived, not merely believed; carried, not merely considered. I found myself grounded in the world God placed me in, yet strangely aware of something beyond it: fully here yet not limited by here.

Signal, Noise, and the Holy Simplicity of Listening

What if connection—what I will often call signal in this book—between God and humanity is not as complicated as we've made it? What if it's profoundly simple, and our problem is not the signal itself but the noise around it? In a world filled with static—constant inputs, constant arguments, constant urgency—could it be that the most radical act is not searching harder, but listening deeper?

This might be why stillness matters so much. "Be still and know that I am God" (Psalm 46:10). **What if stillness is not merely therapeutic, but theological?** Not merely a technique for anxiety, but a posture of attunement? We do not evolve into comprehension of God. Perhaps we surrender into the knowing of Him. Not the knowing that comes from stacking facts, but the knowing that comes from being near enough to recognize His signal beneath the noise.

Creation as Declaration, Not Debate

From the intricacies of cellular design to the fine-tuned constants of the universe, creation bears the marks of intelligence—not as a shouting proof, but as a quiet pattern. Science, when used humbly, often feels less like a threat to faith and more like a spotlight. The more closely we observe, the more reality behaves like something meant to awaken wonder.

This is where science, when it remains humble, can feel like worship. **Science does not author reality; it observes it.** It names patterns already present. It studies obedience already occurring. The "laws of nature" are creation's consistent response to the way it was spoken into being. Maybe that's why the psalmist doesn't say the Heavens argue God into existence. He says they declare. "The Heavens declare the glory of God, and the sky above proclaims His handiwork" (Psalm 19:1). They do not debate. They broadcast.

The Body as an Invitation to Awe

Think about the body for a moment. What if one of the clearest invitations to contemplate the Architect is living right beneath our skin? Your heart keeps time like a drummer in a vast orchestra, contracting and releasing with rhythmic precision. Your nervous system sends electrical signals at speeds you cannot feel, coordinating movement, sensation, memory, and instinct. Your immune system identifies threats with a discernment that feels almost moral recognizing what belongs and what does not. Your cells replicate with stunning fidelity, and when something goes wrong, repair mechanisms work quietly in the background like faithful custodians. Could it be that life itself is a conversation of signals?

And when those signals drift, everything wobbles. If the pH of your blood veers too far in either direction, organs begin to fail. If the electrical rhythm of your heart loses its timing, strength can collapse in seconds. If genetic instructions within a single cell are corrupted beyond repair, the cell either dies or multiplies into disease. What if this fragility is not an argument against design, but a reminder of how finely tuned life is? A symphony does not have to be fragile to be beautiful, but it is fragile in a particular way: it depends on harmony.

The Cosmos as a Whisper of Intent

Zoom out from the body to the cosmos, and the same kind of coherence seems to echo. The universe is held together by constants so delicately balanced that even a slight shift would render life impossible. Gravity must be strong enough to form stars, but not so strong that everything collapses. Electromagnetism must bind atoms together but not bind them so tightly that chemistry cannot happen. The expansion of the universe cannot be too fast or too slow. Is it possible that this fine—tuning is not merely a curious fact, but a whisper of intent? Not a proof we wield like a weapon, but an invitation we receive like a letter.

Maybe this is why Scripture speaks the way it does about creation. "In Him all things hold together" (Colossians 1:17). Could it be that the steadiness we rely on—day after day, law after law, pattern after pattern—is not evidence that God is absent, but evidence that God is faithful? Predictability may look mundane, but perhaps it is holy. "He set the earth on its foundations, so that it should never be moved" (Psalm 104:5). Stability is not accidental. What if order is one of the most underappreciated mercies in existence?

The Limits That Keep Wonder Alive

Still, perhaps we should be honest about the limits. Science can describe how sound travels, but it cannot finally answer why sound exists. It can measure vibration, but it cannot assign ultimate meaning to what is being communicated. It can map resonance, but it cannot determine purpose. These are not failures of science; they are acknowledgments of its domain. "The secret things belong to the LORD our God, but the things that are revealed belong to us" (Deuteronomy 29:29). What if the problem arises when we forget the posture of observation and begin to pretend we are the Author?

Scripture never discourages understanding; it simply refuses to crown it. "Trust in the LORD with all your heart, and do not lean on your own understanding" (Proverbs 3:5). Perhaps the invitation isn't to abandon thought, but to release the illusion of control. Understanding is welcomed. But it is not enthroned.

Blueprint and Boundary

If God is the Architect, then His design would likely reveal intent, not improvisation. And intent often reveals itself through structure. Genesis is full of boundaries and sequences: light and darkness separated, waters gathered, land appearing, living things multiplying "according to their kinds." The text reads like calibration, as if the world is being tuned. Could it be that God is not only making things, but arranging them so that life can flourish? A blueprint is not merely about beauty; it is about function. It is about making a space where something can live.

And yes, the questions still matter. Did God create all things in seven days? Were those literal days or metaphorical epochs of unfolding time? Scripture leaves room for wonder here. God exists outside of time. "With the Lord one day is as a thousand years, and a thousand years as one day" (2 Peter 3:8). But perhaps the deeper question is not about the length of the day. Perhaps it is about the nature of the One who speaks. It is possible to analyze what God did and still miss who God is.

Psalm 103 hints at this distinction: God showed Moses His ways, but Israel His acts (Psalm 103:7). Acts can impress. Ways require relationship. What if Scripture was never intended to function primarily as a technical manual, but as an invitation—to be experienced while interacting with God? Before words were written, they were spoken. Shared. Received. Held in community. The Word began as living communication.

And then there is that repeated phrase—so simple we almost miss its tenderness: "And God saw that it was good" (Genesis 1:10, 12, 18, 21, 25; culminating in Genesis 1:31). What if this is not God grading His work like a critic, but God revealing His heart like a Father? **Architects do not call a structure good simply because it stands. They call it good when it accomplishes its purpose**—when it holds what it was designed to hold, when it shelters what it was designed to protect, when it creates space where life can flourish.

Could it be that "good" is the language of sacred satisfaction? Not pride—something cleaner than that. Something like joy. God pauses to behold what He has made, not because He is uncertain, but because He is attentive. And attention is love. Perhaps "good" is Heaven's way of saying, *This is aligned. This is harmonized. This is ready for life.* And maybe that repeated pause is itself a lesson for us. What if the Architect is showing us that holiness is not only in the creating, but in the *beholding*? In refusing to rush past wonder. In naming what is rightly ordered before moving on to the next thing.

And when the text reaches humanity, the "good" becomes almost luminous. "Let us make man in our image, after our likeness" (Genesis 1:26). The rhythm changes here. It slows. It gathers weight. It is as if the Architect steps closer to the center of His design—not to add another object to the world, but to place within it a being capable of recognition. A creature who will not merely exist within creation's order, but perceive it, respond to it, and reflect the One who made it.

Resonance and the Nature of Relationship

And maybe that matters more than we realize, because sound is relational by nature. Sound assumes a source and a receiver. It moves between. It does not exist as a private possession. When God speaks, perhaps He is not only exerting power; perhaps He is offering relationship. His voice assumes a listener. In Genesis, creation itself becomes the first listener: waters gather, light appears, the earth brings forth. It is as if matter was designed to respond. As if existence itself is receptive.

If creation is receptive, what does that suggest about us? Scripture says we are made in God's image (Genesis 1:26). Could it be that image-bearing includes the capacity to perceive Him? That we were crafted not only to exist inside the design, but to recognize the Designer? Creation declares His glory, and humanity is designed to notice.

In physics, resonance occurs when one vibrating system influences another to oscillate at the same frequency. Strike a tuning fork, and a nearby fork of the same pitch begins to sing. Pluck a guitar string, and a second string quietly answers if it is tuned to the same note. Resonance is not forced; it is awakened when two things are aligned. **So what if faith is not primarily mental agreement, but alignment—becoming tuned to the Voice behind all voices?**

"His voice" is not a poetic idea in Scripture. "He upholds the universe by the word of His power" (Hebrews 1:3). The Word is not static; it sustains. Frequency is not autonomous. Vibration is not self—originating. Creation continues because God continues. Could it be that the universe is still listening, not in a conscious way like a human listens, but in a responsive way—obeying the ongoing command embedded into its being?

Releasing a Human—Shaped God

And perhaps this is where we must begin to release a human—shaped God. When someone asks, "How would you describe God?" many of us instinctively shape Him in the only image we know well—our own. We import our wounds into our theology without realizing it. We take the face of a disappointed parent, the voice of a controlling leader, the cold distance of a neglectful friend, and we paint it onto the Creator. Then we wonder why prayer feels unsafe, why worship feels strained, why faith feels like bracing for impact instead of resting in love.

Scripture interrupts that projection with a steady correction: "God is not a man" (Numbers 23:19). That line doesn't exist to make God feel cold. Perhaps it exists to make God feel clean—to separate Him from our distortions. To release God from a human framework is not to make Him distant; it may be the very thing that makes intimacy possible.

Because intimacy with an imaginary God is ultimately exhausting. You will always be trying to manage Him. **But intimacy with the true God—holy, infinite, unbound—can become the safest kind of love, because it is not built on your projections. It is built on revelation.**

So what does it mean when Scripture says God is not man? Perhaps it is redefining His nature, not denying His nearness. Jesus says plainly, "God is Spirit" (John 4:24). Spirit is not absence; it is fullness without boundaries. God is not confined to physical form, location, or material limitation. He does not occupy space the way bodies do; He permeates it. If that is true, then God is not accessed primarily through physical proximity or sensory certainty, but through alignment—attention, truth, receptivity.

God is also Creator: "In the beginning, God created" (Genesis 1:1). Creator is not just what He does; it is who He is. Everything that exists flows from His initiative, not necessity. He creates not to complete Himself, but to express abundance. "You formed my inward parts; you knitted me together" (Psalm 139:13). What if your existence is not a random occurrence, but a designed expression—an authored life meant to carry meaning?

God is the Life—Giver: "He breathed into his nostrils the breath of life" (Genesis 2:7). In Hebrew, ruach means breath, wind, spirit. Perhaps Scripture is showing us that what sustains us is not only biological, but spiritual—that your every breath is a living reminder of dependence and gift.

God is eternal: "From everlasting to everlasting you are God" (Psalm 90:2). And God is unchanging: "I the LORD do not change" (Malachi 3:6), with "no variation or shadow due to change" (James 1:17). Perhaps that steadiness is what makes rest possible—rest that is not denial but anchoring.

What does the Architect see when He prepares to make man in His own image? We often ask what we are meant to *do*, but perhaps the deeper question is what we are meant to *mirror*. Image—bearing can't mean we are miniature gods, but could it mean we are designed as reflectors—receivers and responders? Not just minds that think, but spirits that perceive. Genesis does not say God constructed humanity like He constructed the stars. It says He formed man with a kind of intimacy—"then the LORD God formed the man of dust from the ground and breathed into his nostrils the breath of life" (Genesis 2:7). **Breath is personal. Breath is near. Breath suggests not distance, but impartation.**

And if we are made in His image, could it be that we are also made in His pattern—as builders? Not builders of galaxies, but builders of what is sacred on earth: lives, homes, words, communities, altars of attention. Scripture speaks of this posture with surprising tenderness: "We are his workmanship, created in Christ Jesus for good works" (Ephesians 2:10). Workmanship implies craft. It implies intention. And it implies that the One who made us understands the making of us from the inside.

Maybe this is why the idea of building shows up again and again in the language of faith. "For every house is built by someone, but the builder of all things is God" (Hebrews 3:4). And later, we are told to "be careful how" we build (1 Corinthians 3:10). As though God is not only the Architect of existence, but the One teaching His children how to build in resonance with Him—how to construct a life that can bear His presence without collapsing under the weight of noise.

So when God calls creation "good," perhaps He is also planting in humanity the desire to build goodness—to recognize order, to hunger for harmony, to ache when things are detuned, and to feel a quiet joy when they are restored. What if that ache is not weakness, but design? What if the longing to create what is beautiful and whole is one of the clearest traces of the Architect's image still pulsing within us?

The World That Sings and Groans

And yet, we cannot ignore that the world is both ordered and wounded. It sings and it groans at the same time. Like a piano with one string slightly off—everything is nearly right, and that's why the dissonance aches. Or like a melody played on an instrument with a warped neck. Bodies break. Relationships fracture. But it still a world in motion, and it's our world. Even the earth itself can feel like a sanctuary one moment and a storm the next. Nature can soothe and it can destroy. We live inside a paradox: beauty that still bears fingerprints of intention, and sorrow that feels like an interruption—an unwanted note that doesn't belong in the score.

Perhaps the presence of brokenness does not erase design; it reveals that something has gone wrong with the harmony. Scripture calls that rupture sin—not merely as moral failure, but as misalignment, a detuning of the human heart from God's life. Sin is not only what we do; it is what we drift into when we refuse the true pitch of Heaven and begin to normalize the static. We settle for counterfeit frequencies—fear, pride, shame, control—until distortion starts sounding like home. The ache we feel when things fall apart is not just grief; it is the soul recognizing dissonance, remembering that this is not how it was meant to sound.

But even in the static, the blueprint persists. The very fact that we call something broken implies we know what "whole" looks like. We carry an inner reference point—an echo of Eden, a memory of alignment—even if we can't fully name it. That's why injustice stings, betrayal burns, and death feels offensive: not only because they hurt, but because they contradict the deep witness within us that life was designed for communion, not fracture. And maybe that is mercy in itself—that our hunger for wholeness has not been removed. It remains as evidence that we were made for harmony and as invitation to return to the One Who holds the original song.

The Architect Enters His Own Architecture

If that is true, then **the Gospel is the most astonishing form of intelligent design: God does not merely build a world; He enters it to restore resonance.** "The Word became flesh and dwelt among us" (John 1:14). What if the Incarnation is the Architect stepping into His own architecture, not as a distant observer, but as Redeemer? The eternal enters time. The Creator steps into creation. The Life—Giver submits to mortality. The Unchanging becomes touchable. In Christ, the Architect is not abstract. He is embodied.

And what does Jesus do with His embodied presence? He speaks, and storms listen. He calls, and graves answer. He touches what is detuned and restores it. Could it be that every miracle is not merely power on display, but harmony being reintroduced? Not spectacle, but signal. The divine sound carried into places where our lives have gone silent.

Perhaps that is the most staggering turn in the story: not that Heaven sent help, but that Heaven came Himself. "The Word became flesh and dwelt among us" (John 1:14). If sin had introduced separation—if it fractured communion and bent the human heart into a looping dissonance—then the remedy could never be mere instruction shouted across the distance. It would require presence. It would require the Maker stepping into the very structure that had been damaged, walking its halls, feeling its weight, bearing its consequences, and restoring what the collapse had threatened to make permanent. "Since the children share in flesh and blood, He Himself likewise also partook of the same" (Hebrews 2:14). Not as a visitor passing through, but as the Architect who loves His architecture enough to enter it and repair it from within.

And what if this is why Jesus is more than a teacher? What if He is, in the deepest sense, the Repairer—of breach, of signal, of resonance? Scripture uses that phrase—"the repairer of the breach" (Isaiah 58:12)—and while its immediate context speaks to restoration in the life of God's people, it also feels like a prophetic echo of Christ's mission: to mend what humanity could not mend, to close what we could not close, to reconnect what we could not reconnect.

We can feel the break in ourselves, can't we? The way we know what is right yet are pulled toward what destroys. The way shame scrambles clarity. The way fear makes us hide from the very Presence we were made to enjoy (Genesis 3:8–9). The signal wasn't lost because God went silent; it was distorted because the receiver was damaged. So the Son came not only to speak truth, but to restore our capacity to hear it—to repair the inner breach where communion had been severed.

This is why fulfillment is not merely legal language; it is architectural language. Jesus said, "Do not think that I came to abolish the Law or the Prophets; I did not come to abolish but to fulfill" (Matthew 5:17). Fulfillment is completion. It is bringing the design to its intended end. The Law revealed what holiness requires, but it could not supply the power to become what it demanded. It could diagnose, but it could not heal. So Christ entered the structure and did what no human could do from the outside: He carried our sin into death and broke its authority at the root. "He Himself bore our sins in His body on the cross" (1 Peter 2:24). "He made Him who knew no sin to be sin on our behalf, so that we might become the righteousness of God in Him" (2 Corinthians 5:21). Death—the ultimate separator—was not merely avoided; it was confronted and conquered.

He rendered powerless the one who held the power of death and delivered those who were enslaved by its fear (Hebrews 2:14–15). The breach that threatened to separate forever was met with a cross that refused to let separation have the final word.

And then came the sign that felt like Heaven's own announcement: the veil was torn. "And behold, the veil of the temple was torn in two from top to bottom" (Matthew 27:51). Not from bottom to top, as though humans clawed their way into God's presence, but from top to bottom—an act initiated from above, a divine declaration that access had been restored. The tearing was not merely dramatic; it was a manifest signal: the barrier is removed. The way is open.

"Therefore, brethren, since we have confidence to enter the holy place by the blood of Jesus… let us draw near with a sincere heart in full assurance of faith" (Hebrews 10:19–22). And if the signal is restored, then the fear of permanent separation begins to lose its grip. "For I am convinced that neither death, nor life… nor any other created thing will be able to separate us from the love of God, which is in Christ Jesus our Lord" (Romans 8:38–39).

So when the world grows loud and His voice seems to dim, perhaps that is not proof of His absence, but a call back to alignment. A reminder that the restoration Christ secured is not fragile, yet our attention can be. We can live as though the veil still hangs, as though distance still rules, as though shame still gets the last word. But the Architect has entered His architecture, and the repair is real. He did not come merely to improve our behavior; He came to restore communion. To reestablish resonance. To make it possible—again—for dust filled with breath to live in clear relationship with the One who breathed in the first place.

The Architect does not remain at a safe distance from His own design. He enters it.

The Invitation Across the Threshold

Perhaps the question becomes personal: if the universe is upheld by the Word, are we trying to uphold our souls by striving? What if the steadiness we seek is not achieved by effort, but received by nearness? Life, in this light, isn't primarily about becoming impressive or superior. Perhaps it is about becoming aligned—letting truth tune us, letting grace recalibrate us, letting presence restore what performance could never fix. Yielding, then, is not loss; it is safety. It is returning to the design you were made for.

Maybe that is the quiet invitation threaded through creation itself. Not that you would conquer the mystery, but that you would inhabit it. **Not that you would reduce God to a conclusion, but that you would recognize Him as the Architect and rest in His order.** Not that you would force yourself into certainty, but that you would become still enough to notice the signal that has been there all along.

If creation truly reflects the mind of an Architect, then the order we observe is not accidental—it is intentional. The stars hold their courses, the oceans keep their boundaries, and life unfolds within patterns that make existence possible.

Every measurement, every rhythm, every law of nature hints at a Designer who understands the structure of life before life even begins. Yet the most remarkable part of that design is not found in galaxies or gravitational constants. It is found in us.

At the center of creation, the Architect forms something unlike the rest of His work—a being made not merely to exist within the design, but to recognize it, interact with it, and bear responsibility within it. In that moment, the story of creation becomes personal.

Enter Adam.

ADAM

Formed From Dust, Filled With Breath

Then comes Adam—not simply as a figure in an ancient story, but as a mirror. After the Architect sets the foundations of creation, Scripture pauses and reveals something astonishing: humanity is formed differently. "Then the LORD God formed the man from the dust of the ground and breathed into his nostrils the breath of life" (Genesis 2:7). Dust becomes alive, not through mechanics, but through breath. In that moment the Creator shares something of Himself with creation. Adam becomes more than a creature within the design—he becomes an image-bearer. And if humanity carries the breath of God, then the story of Adam is not distant history. It is the beginning of our own.

Formed from dust, filled with breath—there is something in that phrase that refuses to behave like a mere origin story. It feels more like a threshold. Dust is humble. Dust is common. Dust gathers where life has moved on. And yet Scripture dares to say that the living God stooped into that ordinary substance and shaped a human frame, then leaned close enough for intimacy and breathed.

We read those words so often that they can sound rehearsed and impersonal. But if we let the scene regain its depth, it becomes almost unbearable in its tenderness. God could have created humanity the way He created so much else: by speaking from a distance. Stars were summoned by command. Oceans were appointed. Trees rose at His word. **But Adam—Adam is breathed. There is closeness here. The God, who is infinite, chooses nearness, as though the first human life must begin not with a decree alone, but with contact.**

And immediately, the mind stirs with questions that feel less like skepticism and more like holy curiosity. "So God created mankind in His own image, in the image of God He created them; male and female He created them" (Genesis 1:27). If God is spirit—"God is spirit, and those who worship Him must worship in spirit and truth" (John 4:24)—then what part of us is truly made in His image? Bone cannot resemble Spirit. Skin cannot mirror Infinity. And yet we are told, without hesitation, that we bear His likeness.

The First Listener

Perhaps the image is not in the material alone, but in what the material has been designed to host. A body made from dust, yes, but dust that becomes a dwelling. Dust that becomes an instrument. Matter fused with a breath that does not originate in matter. In Genesis, the human being is not an accident of chemistry; the human being is a fusion of earth and ruach—breath, wind, spirit (Brown—Driver—Briggs Hebrew Lexicon, "ruach"). The word itself suggests invisible movement with undeniable effects, like wind that cannot be seen but can be felt and traced by what it stirs.

And what if ruach is also more than "air"? What if breath itself is part of the language of God?

Breath is never neutral. Even before a baby learns a single word, the child listens. We come into the world with ears already tuned for voice. Infants recognize cadence, tone, and safety before they can form sentences. They are shaped by what they hear long before they can explain it. The body learns belonging through sound. In that sense, humanity does not begin with speech but with reception. The first posture of life is not output. It is openness.

"Faith comes from hearing, and hearing by the word of Christ" (Romans 10:17). That line is often quoted as a theological principle, but it is also an echo of Eden's design. Faith is not merely the conclusion of an argument; it is the response of a receiver. It arises when something living is heard, received, and recognized. Could it be that God built us this way on purpose? That the human heart is meant to awaken through encounter, not through conquest?

In acoustics, sound is a physical phenomenon—pressure variations traveling as mechanical waves through a medium such as air, water, or tissue (Fletcher & Rossing, *The Physics of Musical Instruments*, 2nd ed., 1998). Sound requires a source, a medium, and a receiver. The waves are unseen, and yet their effects are measurable. What we call "hearing" is the nervous system translating vibration into meaning. In that sense, creation itself is saturated with invisible motion. The world is never truly still.

So when God breathes into Adam, we are not forced to imagine something mystical in a way that denies the physical. We can honor the physical while admitting the mystery. Breath is movement. Movement implies vibration. Breath is a carrier, and carriers can carry more than oxygen.

What if the breath of God imparted more than biological life? What if it established resonance—an inner alignment, a tuning of the human instrument toward its Source? We were not created merely to think, but to behold. And what we behold, we begin to reflect. **Resonance and reflection may be among the most powerful capacities humanity possesses.**

There is a simple demonstration that has startled musicians and physicists for centuries. Strike a tuning fork, and it begins to vibrate at a particular frequency. Hold it near another tuning fork tuned to the same pitch, and the second begins to sing without being struck. Energy transfers through the air, and a silent object awakens because it is tuned to match what is sounding. This is resonance: one oscillating system inducing vibration in another when their natural frequencies align (Halliday, Resnick, & Walker, *Fundamentals of Physics*, 10th ed.).

Adam, then, can be seen as the first listener—created with the capacity to resonate with God because God Himself initiated the vibration. The first human consciousness did not ignite through effort, but through breath received. God breathed, and Adam lived. God spoke, and Adam listened. Before Adam ever named a creature, before He ever shaped language into a sentence, He was a receiver. His life began not by reaching for God, but by being reached.

This posture changes how we understand dominion.

Authority Through Alignment

So much of human history has been a story of domination: power exercised through force, control, fear, and grasping. We have learned to associate "authority" with pressure. But in Eden, authority is not coercion; it is harmony. "The LORD God took the man and put him in the garden of Eden to work it and keep it" (Genesis 2:15). The verbs are not violent. They suggest cultivation, guarding, stewardship. Adam is placed in a garden, not a battlefield. His assignment is not conquest, but care.

Dominion, then, may be less about control and more about agreement. Adam's authority flowed from alignment. As long as He remained tuned to the voice of God, creation responded in peace. This is why naming is so sacred in Genesis. Naming is not merely labeling; it is recognizing the nature of a thing and speaking in agreement with what God has made. Adam's voice was meant to echo God's, not replace it.

"Death and life are in the power of the tongue" (Proverbs 18:21). That proverb can feel dramatic until we admit how true it is. Words shape the interior world of a child. Words can lift a spouse out of despair or press them into it. Words can form a culture, bless a community, fracture a friendship. Our speech does not merely describe reality; it participates in it. And if God created through speech, then humans—made in His image—carry a derivative authority in our speech. Authority was never about volume. It was about alignment.

If Eden is the origin of our assignment, it is also the origin of our atmosphere.

Eden as Atmosphere

Imagine the garden not only as a beautiful place, but as the original environment designed for human formation. According to Scripture, Eden is where God and humanity met without dread. They walked together. They shared presence. There was no temple because the whole space was communion. There were no intermediaries because the relationship was direct. "They heard the sound of the LORD God walking in the garden in the cool of the day" (Genesis 3:8). Notice how the narrative is careful to include the auditory detail. There is a sound associated with God's nearness.

Eden, then, was more than geography. It was an inner condition mirrored by an outer world. It was the kind of place where the nervous system did not live on edge, where the soul did not brace for rejection, where the heart did not rehearse shame. There was no buzzing static of self—protection. No fear of being exposed. Adam and Eve were naked and unashamed (Genesis 2:25). That nakedness is not merely physical; it is spiritual transparency. Nothing to hide. Nothing to prove. Curiosity without suspicion. Creativity without anxiety. Rest without guilt.

It is difficult for us to imagine such simplicity because our inner world is often loud. We live with notifications, expectations, comparisons, unfinished to—do lists, and unhealed memories that replay like broken recordings. We know what it is to hear many voices at once: the voice of fear, the voice of shame, the voice of accusation, the voice of exhaustion. Even our prayers can become crowded. But Eden whispers that humanity was made for clarity.

And then the story breaks, not because God stops speaking, but because humans stop receiving.

After the disobedience, the narrative says they heard God's sound and hid (Genesis 3:8). That one detail is devastating. The same sound that once meant safety now felt unbearable. Something in the inner receiver was detuned. Shame entered. Fear rose. Dissonance appeared, not in God's voice, but in humanity's capacity to resonate with it.

This is a tragedy deeper than exile from a location. It is exile from a way of being.

When God calls, "Where are you?" (Genesis 3:9), He is not asking for coordinates. He is revealing the rupture. He is drawing attention to the broken line between presence and perception. Perhaps that question still reverberates through history, not as accusation, but as invitation. Where are you? Come out from hiding. Return to the open. Return to the sound that made you.

If Eden was the original sound chamber of divine intimacy, then the long story of Scripture is the story of God restoring resonance. The human heart keeps searching for home, and often it searches in the wrong places. We chase comfort, control, applause, spiritual performance, certainty. We attempt to build new Edens out of success or distraction. But the longing remains, because it was never merely a longing for a place. It was a longing for communion.

"He who dwells in the secret place of the Most High shall abide under the shadow of the Almighty" (Psalm 91:1). The "secret place" is not a hidden room God reserves for the spiritually elite. It reads more like an atmosphere—abiding, dwelling, remaining. Jesus uses the same language when He says, "Abide in Me, and I in you…apart from Me you can do nothing" (John 15:4–5). Abiding is not frantic religion. It is proximity. It is staying close enough to hear.

And then there is that command that feels like a hand on the shoulder: "Be still and know that I am God" (Psalm 46:10). The verse does not say, "Be still and understand." It says, "Be still and know." Knowing is relational. Knowing is what happens when the inner noise lowers enough for recognition. Perhaps stillness is not merely the absence of sound; perhaps it is the restoration of signal.

In communication theory, a message travels through a channel with interference. The clarity of reception depends on the signal—to—noise ratio—how much of what arrives is the true message versus the surrounding distortion (Shannon, "A Mathematical Theory of Communication," 1948). Spiritual life is not reducible to engineering, and yet the analogy is helpful. If your life is full of noise, it becomes difficult to discern what is true. **Sometimes the work is not to make God louder, but to become quieter.** To lower the internal static long enough to recognize the Voice that has been present all along.

This is where the body matters more than we realize.

The Body as Conduit, The Fall as Dissonance

"I praise You because I am fearfully and wonderfully made; Your works are wonderful; I know that full well" (Psalm 139:14). That praise is not sentimental; it is accurate. The human body is an instrument—built for breath, vibration, and resonance. The larynx houses the vocal folds, which vibrate as air passes through them, transforming breath into sound (Titze, *Principles of Voice Production*, 1994). Resonance chambers—the throat, mouth, and nasal cavities—shape that sound into a voice with a signature that cannot be duplicated. A sonic fingerprint carried in flesh.

As a vocal coach, I have watched this with awe. A small adjustment in posture changes tone. A release in the jaw changes clarity. A softened breath changes warmth. And when someone finally sings without fear—when breath is free and sound is unashamed—something in the room shifts. The atmosphere changes. People feel it in their bodies. Sound is invisible, but it carries weight.

If we are designed to move sound through flesh, then faith is not meant to be purely mental. The Word was meant to be heard. Spoken. Received. Released. "Hear, O Israel…" (Deuteronomy 6:4). The Hebrew verb shama implies hearing that includes receiving and responding, not mere auditory intake (Brown—Driver—Briggs Hebrew Lexicon, "shama"). In the New Testament, the language of hearing includes *akoē*, and the Word can be framed as *rhēma*—spoken utterance that becomes living when received (BDAG Greek Lexicon, "akoē," "rhēma"). Faith, then, is not passive exposure; it is relational reception.

This is why studying Scripture can feel like reading sheet music in silence if it never becomes sound in us. We can analyze verses, organize doctrines, and still miss the voice. **But when Scripture is spoken with reverence—when it moves through breath and body—something awakens.** The Word is not merely examined; it is received. And reception changes the receiver.

This is also why the Fall is best described as dissonance, not disappearance.

God's voice did not vanish from the world. Humanity's ability to resonate with it was disrupted. We still hear, but not clearly. We still speak, but often out of alignment. We still breathe, but we forget what breath was meant to carry.

And yet, even here, the mercy of God persists. He continues to tune His voice to reach us.

Some people have noticed something tender about the divine Name revealed in Scripture. God tells Moses, "I AM WHO I AM" (Exodus 3:14). The sacred Name associated with this revelation is often rendered YHWH. Throughout Jewish tradition, the Name is treated with awe.

Some teachers have observed that the consonants of the Name can resemble breath sounds, as though the act of breathing itself is a quiet witness. Whether or not one presses that observation linguistically, the theological truth remains: "In Him we live and move and have our being" (Acts 17:28). Life is upheld. Breath is sustained. Existence itself is dependent, moment by moment, on a God who remains present.

What if every inhale is a reminder that we were made to receive?

What if every exhale is an invitation to release what we have received in trust?

This is where an old phenomenon from acoustics becomes a parable for the soul. In cymatics—patterns produced by sound vibrations in a medium—frequency organizes matter into visible geometry. Sand on a plate forms intricate shapes when the plate vibrates. Water responds with ripples and lattices. When the frequency changes, the pattern changes (Jenny, *Cymatics: A Study of Wave Phenomena and Vibration*, Vol. I, 1967). Long before that term existed, Ernst Chladni demonstrated similar patterned forms using vibrating plates and sand (Chladni, *Entdeckungen über die Theory des Klanges*, 1787). The medium receives the vibration, and order appears.

If sound can shape sand into symmetry, what might the voice of God shape in a human life when received without resistance? What patterns of fear might soften? What hardened habits might reorder? What inner chaos might begin to settle into beauty—not by force, but by resonance?

Each human being is a different medium. We carry different histories, different wounds, different temperaments, different longings. The same truth can land differently in different Hearts, not because truth is changing, but because God is personal. His voice is always faithful. His transforming work is always intimate.

Adam, then, is not a relic of ancient history. He is a mirror. He reminds us what humanity was meant to be: receiver, carrier, reflector. Formed from dust, animated by breath, tuned for communion. **Adam also reveals what was lost: not merely a garden, but a frequency of belonging. A state of being unashamed in the presence of God.**

And He hints at what can be found again.

The restoration of resonance often begins in a way that feels almost too simple to be true. Not simple in the sense that pain is trivial. Not simple in the sense that Healing is instant. But simple in its direction. Turn toward the Source. Seek first. "But seek first His kingdom and His righteousness, and all these things will be added to you" (Matthew 6:33). Seeking is not frantic striving; it is orientation. It is letting God be first in attention, first in allegiance, first in desire.

When we begin to seek that way, we start to notice that God has been nearer than we assumed. We recognize Him in Scripture with a sudden brightness, as though a familiar verse carries a new timbre and lands with weight. We recognize Him in creation's order, in the mathematics of petals and the rhythm of tides. We recognize Him in the quiet conviction that is not condemnation but invitation. We recognize Him in worship that feels less like performance and more like coming home.

And sometimes, we recognize Him in our own breath.

Stillness becomes the doorway. Not emptiness, but attentiveness. A willingness to stop hiding from the sound of God. A willingness to let the inner instrument be tuned. There are many moments that the Lord reminds me of the young lady that so enjoyed spending time in worship at the piano, or in prayer in my room or at lunch break at my school. He remembers that I chose stillness when I could have ignored Him. It was in these moments that I was just craving God's presence that He taught me about stillness and being "at peace" with His nearness. There's really no other feeling like it. And today, I know my "secret place" with the

Lord cannot be taken from me. It is the one place I can go to find safety and comfort. I have learned to run towards God for answers and His faithfulness has outlasted many trials and circumstances in my life. I know that I know I can trust the Lord.

The work to be done is on our part, yes—but perhaps it is not as hard as the world, religion, and life would make us think.

In the physics of resonance, the tuning fork does not strain to become the right frequency; it simply is made for it. In the same way, we were designed for communion. We were designed to hear. We were designed to respond. **Tuning in is profoundly simple: return to the One who breathed life into dust and let His voice become the primary sound again.**

Then the rest begins to follow, not as forced achievement, but as the natural overflow of alignment. A new steadiness in the chest. Breath that deepens without being commanded. Courage to be honest. Capacity to bless instead of curse. The quiet strength to steward rather than control. A voice that echoes God's, not as imitation, but as agreement.

God is still speaking. The question is not whether His voice remains, but whether we are willing to listen—receive—and, in time, become its echo.

Faith Comes by Hearing — The Restored Signal of the Kingdom

The more you sit with the pattern of the gospel, the more you begin to notice how deliberately it is built around voice, breath, and reception. The good news does not arrive as mere information to be admired from a distance. It arrives as a living summons that must be heard. It is proclaimed. It is received. It is confessed. It takes residence. "So, faith comes from hearing, and hearing by the word of Christ" (Romans 10:17). That is not just theology—it is architecture. It is the blueprint of restoration: the signal carried by the Word, entering the human receiver through hearing.

And maybe that is the "why" underneath so much of God's design. Hearing comes first because hearing is relational. Hearing requires posture—humility, attention, openness. You cannot truly hear while you are busy proving, performing, or defending. To hear is to yield the illusion of control, even if only for a moment, and let Another speak. When the gospel is preached, it is not simply a message offered; it is a Voice extended. And when that Voice is received, the heart is awakened the way an instrument wakes under the touch of its true frequency. The Gospel does not begin with our reaching; it begins with God's speaking.

Then comes confession—not as a magical formula, but as alignment. Scripture repeatedly connects the receiving of Christ with a personal declaration that agrees with Heaven. "If you confess with your mouth Jesus as Lord and believe in your heart that God raised Him from the dead, you will be saved" (Romans 10:9). This is not salvation by performance; it is salvation by surrender. The mouth becomes a threshold where inner belief meets outward agreement. It is as though God has designed faith to move through the same human channel He built for worship: breath becoming word, word becoming witness, witness becoming belonging.

Confession is not an attempt to persuade God or convince ourselves; it is a deliberate action of the soul aligning from the inside out. In that moment, we agree with Heaven and can come into greater resonance with what God has already done.

And that is exactly why grace stands at the center like an immovable pillar. "For by grace you have been saved through faith; and this is not of yourselves, it is the gift of God; not as a result of works, so that no one may boast" (Ephesians 2:8–9). If salvation were earned, it would be unstable—dependent on the strength of our striving, the purity of our consistency, the perfection of our rituals. But the gospel is not built on our reliability; it is built on Christ's. Our role is not to generate rescue; our role is to receive it. Faith, then, becomes the bridge placed in the gap—not a bridge we engineered, but one we step onto. We trust that

God is still speaking, that His voice can reach us, that His Word is living and active (Hebrews 4:12), and that obedience is not slavery but the natural response of love.

This is where "hearing and obeying" becomes more than moral duty. It becomes the rhythm of life in the Kingdom. The Hebrew idea of hearing—*shama*—carries within it the notion of response, not mere listening. To hear is to receive and to act in agreement with what was heard (Deuteronomy 6:4–5). In the New Testament, Jesus repeatedly links true hearing with doing: "My mother and My brothers are these who hear the word of God and do it" (Luke 8:21). Not because doing earns belonging, but because doing reveals resonance. The tuned heart responds. The awakened receiver echoes what it has received. Obedience becomes the exhale of revelation.

And perhaps this is what it means to inherit rather than achieve. An inheritance is not a paycheck. It is not awarded for labor; it is given because of relationship. We do not earn the Kingdom by rituals, nor do we negotiate our way into it through religious performance. We receive it because the Son has made the way open, and the Father delights to give it. The Kingdom is not primarily a place we reach after death; it is a reality that takes root in the heart now. "The kingdom of God is in your midst" (Luke 17:21, NASB). The King comes near, and His reign begins within.

So, the eternal home we long for may not be merely a destination on a map of the afterlife, but a condition of restored communion—a life resonant with the Divine. To be saved is not simply to be spared; it is to be rejoined. The same Spirit—breath that animated dust in Eden now indwells the believer: "Or do you not know that your body is a temple of the Holy Spirit who is in you…?" (1 Corinthians 6:19). Christ in you, the hope of glory (Colossians 1:27). The signal restored. The veil torn. The Voice not distant but dwelling.

And if that is true, then the most sacred "work" we do is not frantic striving but regular positioning. Returning to the posture of the first listener. Making room again for the Word to be heard. Quieting the noise long enough to recognize the familiar sound of God's presence. We did not initiate this communion, and we cannot sustain it by sheer willpower. But we can choose—again and again—to turn our attention toward Him. To hear. To receive. To speak in agreement with Heaven. And in that cycle—hearing, believing, confessing, obeying—we do not manufacture eternal life; we participate in it.

If humanity was created in the image of God, then Adam represents more than the first man—he represents the beginning of a pattern. The breath placed within him was not merely the start of biological life; it was the beginning of relationship, recognition, and response. Humanity was designed not only to live within creation, but to reflect the Creator who formed it. And throughout Scripture we begin to see that God does not act randomly with His image-bearers. He works through recognizable movements—invitation, testing, encounter, transformation. The story that begins with Adam does not end with Adam. It becomes a pattern God continues to weave throughout human history.

To understand how God forms His people, we must now begin to recognize the Archetype.

Enter Archetype.

ARCHETYPE

Heaven Repeats Itself — Why Scripture Echoes Itself

If God is consistent in His nature, it would make sense that He is consistent in the way He forms His people. Throughout Scripture, certain movements repeat across generations: invitation, wilderness, surrender, encounter, commission. These are not isolated stories scattered across the Bible; they are patterns. The same God who formed Adam continues to shape His image-bearers through recognizable pathways. When we begin to see those patterns clearly, we begin to recognize the Voice behind them.

Once you begin to notice these patterns, they appear everywhere. Abraham is called out of familiarity into promise. Moses is drawn into the wilderness before standing before kings. David is shaped in obscurity before ruling a nation. Even the disciples of Jesus are invited first into relationship before they are sent into mission. The details of each life differ, but the movements feel strangely familiar. God invites. God refines. God reveals. God commissions. These are not random stages of spiritual life—they are the recurring pathways through which the Creator forms those made in His image.

And perhaps the most surprising discovery is this: these patterns are not confined to the pages of Scripture. They continue to unfold in the lives of those who walk with God today. Many people can look back and recognize similar movements in their own journey—moments of calling that disrupted comfort, seasons of wilderness that reshaped priorities, encounters with God that clarified direction, and quiet invitations to step into something greater than themselves. At first these experiences may feel random or even confusing. But when viewed through the lens of God's character, they begin to reveal a deeper order. The same Creator who formed humanity in the beginning still forms His people today, patiently shaping them into reflections of His design.

There is something unmistakable about Scripture once we slow down long enough to actually *hear* it. The Bible does not merely tell a story; it carries a cadence. Themes return. Images reappear. Stories mirror earlier stories with a strange familiarity. At first, if we are reading quickly, we may interpret this as redundancy, as though God is repeating Himself because humanity failed the lesson the first time. But what if repetition is not inefficiency? *What if it is mercy?*

In the natural world, repetition is how formation happens. Muscles are not strengthened by one heroic exertion but by faithful return. Language is not learned in a single explanation but through repeated sounds that slowly become meaning. Music is not acquired by reading notes once; it is carried into the body through listening again and again until the melody becomes instinct. So why would God—who authored the laws of learning, who designed the nervous system, who wired memory into flesh—teach any differently?

Scripture repeats because Heaven speaks in patterns, and patterns are how recognition is born. God is not trying to impress the human mind with originality; He is trying to awaken the human heart with familiarity. We forget, not because we are unintelligent, but because we are distractible. We forget posture. We forget what it feels like to be near. We forget the tone of the voice we once trusted. The same longings return under new pressures, the same fears resurface under new names, and the same temptations arrive dressed in different clothing. And so, God—patient and relational—speaks again.

This is where the word *archetype* begins to take on its rightful weight. In Scripture, archetypes are not clichés, not mythic abstractions, and certainly not symbolic games meant to keep theologians entertained. They are real people and real events that carry enduring meaning because God uses them as repeated revelations of His ways. Moses is not simply a historical leader; He becomes a pattern of deliverance and mediation. David is not simply a king; He becomes a pattern of authority shaped by intimacy. Israel is not only a nation; it becomes a mirror of the human soul—capable of profound devotion, and yet prone to drift.

When Heaven repeats itself, it is as though God is gently asking, *Have you seen this before?* Not so that we can reenact the same story as actors in a religious play, but so that we can recognize where we are listening from in the present moment. **Because the deeper purpose of understanding archetype is not role assignment. It is discernment.**

This is also where worldview quietly shapes belief. Many of us have learned to approach Scripture like a theater of moral sorting. We have been trained to look for heroes and villains, victims and rescuers, so we instinctively ask, "Which character am I?" or "Who is my enemy in this story?" We attach ourselves to the narrative as if Scripture were a wardrobe of spiritual costumes: *Am I David or Goliath? Am I Israel or Egypt? Am I the faithful remnant or the rebellious crowd?*

But Scripture was never written to hand us costumes. It was written to give us clarity. And when we reduce archetypes to moral binaries—good versus evil, right versus wrong, obedience versus punishment—we risk missing the deeper intention. Yes, Scripture names evil. It does not pretend darkness is imaginary. But the center of the biblical story is not conflict; it is communion. The Bible begins not with a battle but with a voice. It begins not with violence but with "And God said." And it culminates not in annihilation but in restoration.

When good versus evil becomes the primary motivator for faith, something subtle happens inside the soul. Fear becomes the engine. Vigilance becomes the posture. We begin relating to God through threat management rather than love. We brace ourselves rather than open ourselves. We strive to perform rather than learn to listen. In that posture, resonance gives way to anxiety, and the signal that was meant to draw us into communion becomes distorted by internal noise.

But when we realize Heaven repeats itself not to escalate conflict but to deepen invitation, the entire Bible begins to sound different. The Old Testament is no longer a set of stories we "graduate from." It becomes a patient preparation of perception. Patterns are introduced before they are completed. Shadows appear before substance. The law reveals structure; grace reveals fulfillment. Sacrifice foreshadows restoration. Kingship anticipates servanthood. Temple points toward presence. And then Christ stands at the center, not as a contradiction, but as the resolution—fulfilling the pattern rather than erasing it.

Scripture echoes because God is patient enough to speak again. And if the Bible repeats itself, perhaps the question is not, "Why does it do that?" but rather, "What is this pattern asking me to notice right now?" Heaven is not trapping us in cycles. Heaven is awakening us within them. Suddenly we realize the story we've been born into. It has been written long before we arrived. We're just here to tune into it.

A Glimpse Through Cymatics – where sound reveals pattern

One of the most fascinating modern demonstrations of pattern emerging from invisible forces comes from a field of study known as **cymatics**.

In cymatic experiments, sound frequencies are directed through a medium—often a metal plate dusted with sand or a shallow dish of water. As the plate vibrates, the particles scattered across its surface begin to move. (Skip over to the End Notes section of this book to find some links on YouTube of some videos about cymatics.)

At first the motion appears chaotic, but within moments something remarkable occurs: the particles gather themselves into intricate geometric formations.

The patterns are not random.

Each frequency produces a distinct and repeatable structure. Change the pitch, and the geometry changes with it. Increase the frequency, and the shapes grow increasingly complex—symmetrical forms emerging where moments before there was only scattered dust.

The particles themselves are not deciding where to move. They are responding to the structure of the vibration moving through them. What appears to the eye as beauty is simply matter arranging itself along the stable pathways of the wave.

Cymatics offers a visible reminder of something already true throughout the physical world: Energy organizes matter.

Sound waves carry energy through space, and when that energy encounters a material system, the particles within that system respond. They move toward equilibrium within the wave field, settling into patterns defined by the frequency itself. The result is order emerging from an invisible force.

In this way cymatics reveals something profound about the nature of the world we inhabit. The patterns we see are not imposed from the outside; they are the natural consequence of underlying laws woven into creation.

Invisible shapes visible form.

What cannot be seen exerts influence over what can.

This glimpse into the unseen world at work became the catalyst for a deeper question: what is the impact of God's voice on His creation? That question ultimately gave rise to this book.

I do not present this as "proof" in the scientific sense. Science, by its nature, can only measure and validate systems that already exist—while God exists beyond those systems. And yet, the parallels between how God moves and how creation responds are too consistent to ignore.

What emerges is not proof, but revelation.

When viewed through this lens, the patterns within creation begin to echo the patterns within Scripture. The power, order, and authority of God's voice are no longer abstract ideas—they become observable, recognizable. Again and again, Scripture reveals a God who speaks, and matter responds; who declares, and reality forms.

Once you begin to see it, you cannot unsee it.

What was once distant becomes tangible. What was once theoretical becomes experiential. And what was once read on a page begins to resonate as living truth—pointing not to the system itself, but to the One who set it in motion.

For centuries philosophers and theologians have reflected on this same principle. The physical world is not chaotic at its core; it is structured by intelligible laws that consistently produce order. Whether we observe the formation of crystals, the orbit of planets, or the resonance of sound across a vibrating surface, the same truth appears again and again:

Cymatics does not prove theological claims on its own, but it offers a striking illustration of how unseen forces can generate structure and harmony within the material world.

Matter responds to energy.
Form follows frequency.
And when the right vibration enters a system, chaos gives way to pattern.

The invisible shapes the visible.

"Scripture captures this reality in its own language: **"**By the word of the Lord the heavens were made." — Psalm 33:6

Creation itself bears the signature of the Voice that called it into being.

The Cyclical Nature of Creation

In the cyclical nature of creation—the rhythms we see sustaining life, seasons, breath, and even the movements of faith—it becomes difficult to ignore a deeper consistency at work. Scripture repeatedly presents God as one who establishes order and then remains faithful to the order He has spoken into existence. What He releases does not dissolve into randomness; it continues to move according to His design.

This makes certain passages of Scripture resonate with fresh clarity. When God declares through Isaiah, *"My word that goes out from my mouth will not return to me empty but will accomplish what I desire and achieve the purpose for which I sent it"* (Isaiah 55:11), the statement is not merely poetic reassurance. It describes a principle woven into the fabric of creation itself. Once a word is spoken by God, it carries intention. It moves outward with purpose, accomplishing the work for which it was released.

In the natural world we see something strikingly similar. When energy enters a system—whether through vibration, sound, or frequency—it begins interacting with the matter around it. Particles respond. Structures reorganize. Patterns emerge. The wave does not abandon its nature midway through its movement; it continues to propagate according to the laws that govern it. The system responds because the signal remains consistent.

Scripture describes God in much the same way: not as a being who constantly alters His nature, but as one whose character remains unwavering. *"I the Lord do not change"* (Malachi 3:6). His faithfulness is not only moral—it is structural. The patterns He establishes endure because He Himself remains constant.

This does not mean God is static or distant. Rather, it means His purposes are trustworthy. When Heaven releases a word, a promise, or a pattern into the world, it does not lose coherence as time passes. The signal remains steady. What changes is often the receiver—our attention, our alignment, our ability to recognize the voice that first spoke.

Seen this way, the repeating patterns throughout Scripture begin to make deeper sense. God is not reinventing His ways with every generation. He is revealing the same character through unfolding movements of history, each echo reinforcing what was spoken from the beginning.

The Word moves forward.
The pattern remains consistent.
And creation continues responding to the voice that formed it.

Types, Shadows, and Signals — How God Teaches Through Pattern

One of the sacred mysteries of God's teaching is that He often forms us long before He explains what He is forming. Scripture is not written as a textbook that drops conclusions at the beginning and expects us to memorize them. It is written as a living revelation, unfolding over time, where understanding grows through repeated encounter. God introduces truth in lived form before He names it in language, allowing humanity to dwell inside patterns—sometimes for generations—before unveiling what those patterns were preparing us to recognize.

This is why the Bible feels layered rather than linear. Meaning does not arrive all at once; it ripens. And Scripture itself tells us that this is intentional: "The law is only a shadow of the good things that are coming—not the realities themselves" (Hebrews 10:1). In God's economy, truth is not rushed. It is revealed relationally.

These archetypal patterns appear throughout Scripture in what theologians often call types and shadows—moments where a real event carries meaning beyond itself. Genesis establishes this method immediately. Creation itself is not presented as a scientific breakdown but as a patterned revelation. Light appears before form. Order precedes function. Breath precedes activity. God does not pause to argue His logic; He demonstrates a rhythm of reality: He speaks, creation responds, life aligns. Creation becomes the first archetype, the first template, the first signal of how Heaven and earth relate.

Adam emerges within this rhythm as more than "the first man." He is a patterned man—formed from dust, animated by breath, and given authority through alignment. Yet Adam also reveals the fragility of that alignment. When communion breaks, authority distorts. The signal remains, but the receiver falters. And this prepares us for the truth Scripture later makes explicit: humanity does not need more instruction; humanity needs restoration.

This is why Paul writes, "The first man Adam became a living being; the last Adam became a life—giving spirit" (1 Corinthians 15:45). Adam was never merely a failure to be erased. He was a shadow pointing toward fulfillment.

The Exodus carries the same pattern. God delivers Israel from Egypt before they understand covenant. He parts the sea before they receive the law. He leads them by fire and cloud before the fullness of His nature is articulated. God acts first; understanding follows. And then comes Passover—one of the clearest signals in all of Scripture. Blood on the doorposts. Death passing over. Life preserved through substitution. At the time, Israel cannot fully articulate the theology of what is happening. But the pattern is planted into the bloodstream of their memory.

Centuries later, when John the Baptist points at Jesus and says, "Behold, the Lamb of God, who takes away the sin of the world" (John 1:29), recognition becomes possible. The lamb was never the destination. It was the signal.

Then comes the tabernacle—an architectural sermon built in the wilderness. God gives Moses instructions with astonishing detail: materials, measurements, placement, progression. But this precision is not about aesthetics; it is about approach. The movement from outer court to inner court to Holy of Holies reveals a pattern of nearness. Sacrifice gives way to cleansing, which leads to presence. Form precedes fullness.

So, when John writes, "The Word became flesh and dwelt among us" (John 1:14), the Greek is almost startling: He *tabernacled* among us. The tent becomes a person. The structure was always pointing toward a dwelling that would breathe.

Even the storyline of kingship is a shadow. Saul reveals authority without listening—power detached from intimacy. David reveals a different posture: a king who listens before he rules, a worshiper before He governs. And yet even David points beyond himself. "Your throne shall be established forever" (2 Samuel 7:16) does not ultimately find fulfillment in Solomon. It finds fulfillment in Christ.

Jesus redefines kingship entirely. "The Son of Man did not come to be served, but to serve" (Mark 10:45). The crown was a shadow. The cross reveals the truth beneath it.

God teaches through pattern not because He is cryptic, but because truth received too early becomes law instead of life. He tutors the heart, not merely the mind. Types and shadows preserve mystery while preparing recognition. **And this matters deeply for *The Sound of God*, because sound is not learned through one explanation; it is known through repetition. The signal grows clearer as the ear becomes trained.**

Christ as the Perfect Archetype

When patterns repeat long enough, the soul begins to sense that they are pointing somewhere. It is as if Scripture is patiently building toward a coherence it refuses to rush. Leaders rise and fall. Covenants are established and broken. Sacrifices are offered again and again.

Restoration is promised, glimpsed, tasted—and yet never fully completed. The repetition is not proof of failure. It is preparation.

This is why the Old Testament is not a discarded draft, and the New Testament is not a contradiction. Scripture unfolds like a single composition written in movements. What begins as outline becomes form. What appears first as shadow eventually meets substance. Jesus does not interrupt the story. He completes it.

"Do not think that I have come to abolish the Law or the Prophets; I have not come to abolish them but to fulfill them" (Matthew 5:17). Fulfillment does not mean negation. It means realization. A seed is not contradicted by the tree it becomes.

By this point the pattern becomes unmistakable. The archetypes Scripture introduces across centuries begin to converge in one person: Christ. Christ arrives as the second Adam, not to shame the first, but to restore what was lost. "For as in Adam all die, so in Christ all will be made alive" (1 Corinthians 15:22). Moses reveals deliverance and mediation, ascending the mountain and descending with words. Yet Moses cannot enter the Promised Land, and the pattern remains incomplete. Christ becomes the mediator who does not merely carry the Word—He *is* the Word made flesh.

David reveals kingship shaped by intimacy, yet even David fractures under sin and consequence. His throne cannot remain forever. Christ arrives as king and refuses domination. His authority is not asserted; it is recognized. His crown appears only after the cross.

And the sacrificial system, with its relentless repetition, reveals both longing and limitation. "It is impossible for the blood of bulls and goats to take away sins" (Hebrews 10:4). Sacrifice was never the destination. It was the signal. Christ does not bring another offering. He brings completion. "We have been made holy through the sacrifice of the body of Jesus Christ once for all" (Hebrews 10:10).

Here is the hinge: Christ is not merely a better example within the pattern. He is the pattern resolved. **Where earlier archetypes reveal humanity's response to God, Christ reveals God's response to humanity.**

This matters because faith can quietly turn Jesus into a moral role model rather than a life to receive. We begin to treat Him as the ultimate "how—to," we engage in what I call "self-help Christianity," and the archetype collapses into performance. The pattern becomes pressure. Relationship becomes responsibility.

But Scripture does not present Christ as a role we must play. It presents Him as a life we are invited to enter. "Christ in you, the hope of glory" (Colossians 1:27). The perfect archetype is not perfection as achievement; it is perfection as union. He does not merely show alignment; He restores alignment itself. **He does not demand resonance; He creates it.**

When Christ becomes the center, the storyline shifts. Good versus evil is real, but it is not central. Communion is. Evil is addressed as a consequence of separation, not the center of the narrative. In Christ, Heaven is not escalating the battle; Heaven is resolving the distance.

Cycles of Awakening and Drift — Why Humanity Keeps Relearning

If Christ fulfills the pattern, a natural question follows: why does humanity keep repeating the cycle? Why do seasons of clarity give way to confusion? Why does awakening fade into forgetfulness? Why does revelation feel luminous one moment, then distant the next?

Scripture does not avoid these questions. It acknowledges them with almost tender realism. Humanity does not move through faith in a straight line. We move in cycles. Awakening is followed by familiarity.

Intimacy gives way to distraction. Alignment drifts—not because truth changes, but because attention does.

This is not evidence of failure; it is evidence of formation.

From the earliest pages, the rhythm appears: God reveals Himself, the people respond, life flourishes, remembrance dulls, substitutes emerge, and God speaks again. The prophets are rarely sent to introduce a novelty. They are sent to restore attention—to call the people back to what they already knew but stopped listening to.

"Remember," God says again and again. And remembrance in Scripture is not merely mental recall; it is relational awareness. To forget God is not to lose data about Him. It is to drift from attentiveness to His presence.

Even the disciples lived inside this cycle. They heard Jesus repeat Himself and still misunderstood. They watched miracles and still panicked in storms. They confessed belief and still scattered under pressure. And Jesus, astonishingly, does not respond with contempt. He returns. He speaks again. He restores relationship before correcting perception. Clarity deepens through repetition, not intensity.

Modern spirituality often treats awakening as a singular dramatic event—a lightning strike that should permanently alter the soul. Scripture presents awakening as progressive. It unfolds. It matures. It must be revisited. This is why faith rooted only in emotional moments eventually fades, but faith rooted in rhythm endures.

Drift does not usually begin with rebellion. It begins with distraction. We become occupied. Familiarity replaces wonder. Sacred things become assumed. We still believe, but we no longer listen closely. We still speak God's name, but we no longer pause to hear His voice.

The signal does not disappear; the receiver loses clarity.

Adam's Pitfalls and Promises…

We "break the signal" with God less like we cut a cable, and more like we introduce interference—noise, distortion, misalignment. Scripture's language for this is often relational: drifting, hardening, hiding, dullness of hearing. The voice is steady. The receiver wavers.

The most common ways we weaken the signal are surprisingly human.

Drifting faith…

We hide. Not always physically, but internally—like Adam and Eve when "they heard the sound of the LORD God… and they hid" (Genesis 3:8). Shame makes us withdraw. It convinces us that exposure is danger, so we build distance and call it wisdom. We stop praying with honesty. We stop listening because we're afraid of what He might say, or afraid He might say nothing at all.

We crowd the channel. Life gets loud—not just with external noise, but with inner noise: anxiety, mental rehearsal, comparison, outrage cycles, constant input. Jesus warned that "the worries of the world… and the desires for other things enter in and choke the word" (Mark 4:19). Choking is a signal problem. The seed is living; the environment is crowded. The Word arrives, but it can't breathe.

We harden through repeated resistance. Scripture names this plainly: "Today if you hear His voice, do not harden your Hearts" (Hebrews 3:15; Psalm 95:7–8). A heart hardens the way a path hardens—by many feet walking the same refusal. The most dangerous static isn't a sudden fall; it's slow, ordinary disobedience that trains the soul not to respond.

We substitute information for communion. We can study God the way someone studies sheet music—accurate, impressive, untouched. Jesus said, "You search the Scriptures because you think that in them you have eternal life; and it is these that testify about Me; and you are unwilling to come to Me so that you may have life" (John 5:39–40). **The signal is not merely content; it is Presence.**

We rely on performance instead of grace. Religion can become a self—powered attempt to maintain connection by effort. But connection is received, not earned: "By grace you have been saved through faith… not as a result of works" (Ephesians 2:8–9). Works make us boast or burn out—either way, the channel fills with self. Grace quiets us enough to hear again.

We cling to unforgiveness. Unforgiveness is like spiritual feedback—an endless loop that keeps replaying injury until it becomes identity. Jesus ties forgiveness to our relational openness with the Father (Matthew 6:14–15). Forgiveness doesn't excuse evil; it releases your heart from being permanently tuned to the offense.

We agree with counterfeit voices. The serpent's strategy was not simply temptation; it was distortion—misrepresenting God's character, planting suspicion, reframing the Father as withholding (Genesis 3:1–5). When we start believing God is distant, disappointed, or unsafe, we interpret His silence as rejection and His correction as threat. Then even true guidance can feel like condemnation.

So how do we return? Not by shouting louder, but by recentering the receiver. **Scripture's pathway back is consistent: repent, return, be still, abide, obey.**

We return through honest repentance—realignment, not self—hatred. Repentance is not groveling; it's turning. "Repent… and return, so that your sins may be wiped away, in order that times of refreshing may come from the presence of the Lord" (Acts 3:19). Refreshing implies breath again. Air in the lungs. Signal clearing.

We return through stillness and attention. "Be still and know that I am God" (Psalm 46:10). Stillness is not emptiness; it's uncluttered presence.

It is choosing one Voice over many. It's the discipline of lowering the world's volume so the Kingdom's whisper becomes audible.

We return through Scripture as living speech, not mere text. "Man shall not live on bread alone, but on every word that proceeds out of the mouth of God" (Matthew 4:4). Notice: proceeds. Ongoing. When Scripture is received as God speaking now—especially in prayerful reading—it becomes like fresh bread, not archived history.

We return through confession and worship—breath given back to God. "If you confess with your mouth Jesus as Lord… you will be saved" (Romans 10:9). Confession is alignment. Worship is alignment. Not performance, but agreement: "God inhabits the praises of His people" (Psalm 22:3). Praise recalibrates the heart away from self and back toward the Source.

We return through obedience in small things. Jesus makes it plain: "If anyone loves Me, He will keep My word… and We will come to him and make Our dwelling with him" (John 14:23). Obedience is not how we earn love; it's how love becomes habitable. A life that says "yes" becomes a clearer channel.

We return through abiding—staying close long enough to be changed. "Abide in Me… apart from Me you can do nothing" (John 15:4–5). Abiding is not intensity; it's consistency. It's a thousand quiet returns. It's the soul learning to live in communion instead of visiting God only in emergencies.

And all of it is held together by a single, deeply comforting truth: the burden of reconnection is not on your perfection. It's on His pursuit. The Shepherd goes after the sheep (Luke 15:4–7). The Father runs toward the returning son (Luke 15:20). We weaken the signal in very human ways, yes—but grace is stronger than our interference. Our part is not to manufacture a voice. Our part is to come out of hiding, turn our face toward the Sound, and let the One who breathed life into dust tune us again.

Distorted Faith…

Drift is one thing. Distortion is another. Drift is a gradual loss of attentiveness. **Distortion is when the signal itself becomes misrepresented inside our inner world**. Over time, many of us have inherited frameworks that train us to engage God primarily through fear, combat, performance, or certainty. These frameworks are not entirely false, but when they become dominant, they distort the posture of communion.

When faith is framed primarily as a battle to win, God becomes a commander to appease or a judge to satisfy rather than a Creator to commune with. Awareness tightens. Fear replaces wonder. Vigilance replaces rest. When performance replaces presence, we measure spiritual health by output rather than alignment, by what we do for God instead of how deeply we are attuned to Him. Prayer becomes production. Worship becomes demonstration. Obedience becomes transaction. The soul grows tired—not because God is harsh, but because we have replaced revelation with effort.

An era of deconstructing Christianity…

Many are drawn toward "deconstructing" their faith right now because they are no longer convinced by the evidence the Church has offered about Christ. When what is presented feels insufficient, misaligned, or even harmful, the natural response is to begin pulling it apart.

But this often leads to a deeper problem: attempting to interpret Scripture apart from the Spirit of God who reveals it.

This is where distortion begins.

I am not here to defend the Church's witness—whether it has been faithful or flawed. Instead, I want to point you to the deeper issue beneath the search itself: God's truth cannot be discovered through analysis alone. It is revealed through relationship. Not mediated by a pulpit. Not borrowed from a podcast. But encountered personally, through His Spirit.

I was once given a vision that brought this into sharp focus. I saw people approaching the Bride of Christ and pulling pieces of flesh from her body. It was disturbing—grievous. I could feel the pain of it. And I sensed the Lord say: *this is what deconstruction is doing to My Bride.* In trying to examine and dismantle what has been misunderstood, we often make matters worse—creating not clarity, but further distortion.

Faith cannot be fully grasped through observation alone. And when we attempt to define it apart from revelation, even our conclusions—however sincere—can deepen the confusion.

So if you find yourself in this place, my invitation is not condemnation, but realignment.

Let God reveal Himself to you.

Forgive those who misrepresented Him—those who wounded you, confused you, or led you away from what is true. Your questions are valid. Your pain is real. None of that should be dismissed. But do not let what was broken cause you to reject what is true.

Do not lose the opportunity for personal revelation because of someone else's distortion.

If the image of God you carry feels fractured, understand this: God Himself is not your problem. He has been misrepresented—sometimes deeply, sometimes painfully. And yes, it has left its mark.

But He is not who you've been shown.

He is restoring what has been distorted. He is purifying His house—not to reject His people, but to make room for truth to dwell clearly again. To bring us back to His voice, unfiltered and undistorted.

Let that voice become louder than all the others.

He will speak to you.

I know, because He spoke to me.

There is another subtle distortion as well—one that often hides behind confidence: certainty without communion.

When being right becomes more important than remaining receptive, we quietly close ourselves off to continued revelation. Mystery begins to feel threatening. Questions begin to feel unsafe. But Scripture reveals a God who speaks progressively, relationally, and often in ways we did not expect.

To cling to rigid certainty is to hold onto a static signal, when a living voice is still speaking.

And He is still inviting you to hear Him.

Borrowed Faith…

Then there is borrowed faith—living on someone else's encounter rather than cultivating our own listening. We repeat language we did not receive firsthand. We quote truths we have not yet embodied. Testimony is powerful, but faith cannot be sustained indefinitely by secondhand resonance. Eventually the signal weakens, not because it is untrue, but because it was never fully received.

And perhaps the most pervasive distortion of all is noise disguised as devotion. Constant activity. Constant input. Constant explanation. In a world saturated with spiritual commentary, it is easy to confuse volume for clarity. Yet God has never required constant sound to communicate. Again and again, Scripture reveals that His voice is most clearly discerned in stillness.

The solution is not to shame ourselves for drifting. The solution is to return—not with guilt, but with recalibration. Christ does not stand outside the cycle demanding consistency. He enters it. He remains present in both clarity and confusion.

Faith is not the absence of drift; it is the willingness to return. And every return strengthens resonance.

Recognizing the Pattern— Discernment Through Resonance

If patterns repeat, then discernment is not about prediction; it is about recognition. Scripture does not ask us to master every archetype or map every cycle. It invites us to become attentive to where we are within the pattern. Discernment, in this sense, is not intellectual sharpness or dramatic spiritual insight. It is sensitivity. It is resonance. It is the quiet ability to sense alignment—or its absence—within the soul.

We often assume discernment must arrive like a lightning bolt: a sudden certainty, a vivid supernatural impression, a clean dividing line between right and wrong. But Scripture presents discernment as something subtler and more relational. It grows out of listening. It matures through familiarity with God's tone.

This is why Jesus says repeatedly, "Those who have ears to hear, let them hear." The invitation appears again and again not because Hearing is rare, but because true hearing requires attention. Discernment begins when we notice what we are responding to without realizing it. What stirs urgency in us? What produces fear? What pulls us into striving? What makes our inner world tighten? And conversely, what produces peace that is not denial, rest that is not laziness, clarity that is not forced? These responses reveal the pattern we are currently inhabiting.

When we are aligned, faith feels spacious. Obedience flows as response rather than obligation. We may still face hardship, but we are not internally fragmented by it. Presence steadies us. Even questions feel safe because they are held inside relationship.

When we are drifting, the opposite often occurs. Faith becomes noisy. We feel pressured to do more, prove more, know more. Anxiety masquerades as conviction. Activity replaces attentiveness. We may still believe all the right things, yet something within us feels slightly out of tune.

This is not condemnation. It is information.

The soul often signals dissonance long before the mind can name it. Restlessness, exhaustion, irritation, numbness—these are not necessarily signs of rebellion. They may be invitations to recalibrate. Discernment through resonance means learning to trust these internal cues—not as final authority, but as indicators that we have drifted from the clear channel of communion.

This is where the archetypal patterns become deeply personal. We begin to recognize familiar movements: awakening followed by busyness, clarity followed by control, intimacy followed by explanation. We see ourselves in the story not as heroes or villains, but as learners who are repeatedly invited back to presence.

And the goal is not to escape the pattern but to become conscious within it.

This is why Scripture calls us, again and again, to abide, to remain, to dwell. These are not passive words. They describe sustained attentiveness. They describe staying where the signal is clear. "Be still and know that I am God." Stillness is not inactivity; it is receptivity. It is the posture that allows discernment to emerge without force.

And Here is the grace woven through every pattern: recognition itself is already a form of return. The moment you notice dissonance, alignment becomes possible. The moment you sense drift, recalibration begins. God does not wait for perfection to speak. He responds to attentiveness.

Discernment, then, is not mainly the question, "Am I right or wrong?" It is the question, "Am I listening—and to whom?" That question does not accuse. It awakens. It opens the door back into communion. Heaven repeats itself not to trap humanity in endless return, but to invite us into deeper recognition. And when recognition happens, something quiet but powerful shifts. We ***stop striving*** to stay aligned, and we ***learn how to listen.*** Listening becomes the doorway back into communion, because communion is not maintained by intensity—it is maintained by attentiveness.

In the end, the truest invitation of archetypes is not, "Which pattern do you resemble?" but "Which voice are you responding to?" Every pattern in Scripture—an altar of remembrance, a wilderness that reveals the heart, a table prepared in the presence of enemies—is quietly asking the same question: will you return to the sound that formed you?

Because once you recognize the pattern, you begin to recognize the Voice behind it.

Something subtle but profound happens: our perspective changes. Moments that once felt random begin to reveal intention. Seasons of waiting, wilderness, or uncertainty start to look less like detours and more like formation. The God who shaped Abraham, Moses, David, and the disciples has not changed, and the pathways through which He forms His people have not disappeared.

What once appeared to be scattered stories in Scripture now begins to look like a living pattern still unfolding in the world today. And when a person finally sees that pattern clearly, the realization is both humbling and exhilarating. Because the moment you recognize the pattern… you begin to recognize the Voice behind it.

"My sheep hear my Voice, and they follow Me." – John 10:27

This is the beginning of Awakening.

Enter your Awakening.

AWAKENING

From Information to Revelation — The Moment the Signal Becomes Personal

Awakening rarely begins with a dramatic moment. More often it begins quietly—with a growing awareness that something deeper is happening beneath the surface of ordinary life. What once appeared random begins to reveal intention. Scriptures that once felt familiar begin to carry new weight. Questions that once lingered unanswered start to open into understanding. It is not that God suddenly begins speaking; it is that we begin hearing differently. The patterns that were always present begin to come into focus, and the soul slowly realizes that the Creator has been nearer than it ever imagined.

As awakening unfolds, the world itself begins to look different. Not because creation has changed, but because our perception has. Moments that once felt ordinary begin to carry quiet significance. A verse of Scripture lingers longer than expected. A question rises in the heart that refuses to be dismissed. Even silence begins to feel inhabited. ***Awakening does not force certainty; instead, it opens attentiveness.*** The soul becomes less concerned with managing answers and more willing to listen. And in that listening, a new awareness begins to grow—that God has been present, patient, and speaking in ways we were only beginning to notice.

And as this awareness deepens, something within the heart begins to respond. Awakening does not merely illuminate the mind; it stirs the soul. A quiet reverence begins to replace casual familiarity. The Creator is no longer perceived as distant or abstract, but near—present within the very fabric of life. What once felt ordinary now carries the weight of wonder. The same voice that spoke creation into existence begins to feel personal, as though the One who set the stars in motion is also attentive to the movements of the human heart. And when that realization begins to settle within us, awakening becomes more than awareness. It becomes invitation. Something deeper begins to hunger. And the hunger is not for novelty. It is for encounter.

Scripture names this tension without apology, warning that it is possible to God's words and yet remain unchanged by them: "They seeing see not; and hearing they hear not, neither do they understand" (Matthew 13:13). That sentence is not an insult; it is a diagnosis. Proximity is not the same as participation. Awakening requires more than exposure. It requires consent. It is the moment the heart stops negotiating and simply opens—when the search becomes less about acquiring certainty and more about surrendering to truth, even if truth is costly.

The pages that follow move intentionally into observation. Not to replace revelation, but to notice the ways creation behaves when it is designed to receive, interpret, and respond. The Bible never portrays creation as silent. "The Heavens declare the glory of God; the skies proclaim the work of his hands. Day unto day uttered speech" (Psalm 19:1–2). Creation speaks—not with propositions, but with patterns. Not with doctrine, but with design. If you have ever stood under a night sky and felt your thoughts become small and your wonder become wide, you have tasted what Scripture means. Something in you recognized glory without being able to measure it.

Science, then, is not presented here as a judge of truth, nor as a rival to Scripture. It is a witness. Its role is not to prove God, but to observe what exists and name how it functions. Scripture remains the authority by which meaning is discerned. Yet Scripture itself affirms that what God has made carries testimony: "For since the creation of the world God's invisible qualities… have been clearly seen, being understood from what has been made" (Romans 1:20). To observe is not to exalt the observer. It is to acknowledge that the work already speaks.

Still, observation alone is insufficient. Facts can inform without transforming. Data can accumulate without awakening the soul. The apostle Paul draws this line sharply: "The natural man receives not the things of the Spirit of God… because they are spiritually discerned" (1 Corinthians 2:14). Insight may illuminate design, but only the Spirit reveals meaning. Where observation aligns with Scripture, it supports. Where it strains against it, Scripture corrects. This chapter is not an argument to be won. It is a posture to be entered. If God speaks, the question is not whether sound exists, but whether the listener is attuned. Awakening begins when the signal is no longer external information, but personal revelation.

Awakening is not the moment God begins speaking—it is the moment we begin recognizing His frequency.

Hearing Versus Knowing — Why awareness isn't transformation

Communication, whether expressed through living systems or human—designed technologies, often begins in simplicity and moves toward intelligibility. We casually say, "I hear you," as though hearing is merely passive intake. Yet what we call hearing is a choreography of physics and flesh. When a sound is released—the pluck of a string, the hush of wind, the tremor of a human voice—it sends vibration outward, compressing and releasing the air in traveling waves until it meets the ear. But the ear does not simply receive. It participates.

Inside the cochlea, thousands of microscopic hair cells respond to narrow bands of vibration, converting movement into electrical impulses. Those impulses travel along the auditory nerve into the brain, where another layer of wonder begins. The brain does not hear meaning directly. It receives patterns—timing, amplitude, rhythm—that the mind learns to recognize as meaning. In milliseconds, you identify a voice. You sense danger. You remember a melody that stirs longing or grief. Hearing, in other words, is already interpretive. Even in the natural world, sound is not just received; it is processed, translated, recognized.

Scripture has always insisted on this distinction. Jesus does not merely say hear—He says, "Take Heed therefore how ye hear" (Luke 8:18). The issue is not exposure to sound, but the condition of the listener. A sentence can reach the ear and never reach the heart. We have all experienced this in human relationships: someone speaks with sincerity, and yet if our defenses are high, their words land like pebbles on armor. The same sound is present, but the same sound does not enter.

This is why James writes, "Be ye doers of the word, and not hearers only, deceiving your own selves" (James 1:22). There is a deception that comes from familiarity. You can sit under the sound of truth so long that you begin to confuse recognition with obedience. You nod at what is true. You underline what is beautiful. You repeat what is inspiring. And then you return to patterns that contradict what you just affirmed. **Awareness alone is not transformation. Information alone does not renew.**

Biblically speaking, knowing is never passive. To know is to recognize, to respond, to enter relationship. Scripture uses knowing as the language of union, not merely the language of comprehension. That is why Jesus can say, "You shall know the truth, and the truth shall make you free" (John 8:32). Truth does not liberate because it is heard, but because it is received—received so deeply that it begins to reorder desire, reshape habit, and interrupt old loyalties. Freedom is not merely an idea you agree with; it is a life you come into alignment with.

Perhaps this explains why awakening often feels slower than we want. We assume that if we learn enough, we will become different. But the mind can collect new ideas while the soul remains loyal to old loves. You can study grace and still punish yourself with shame. You can speak fluently about forgiveness and still rehearse offenses in the dark. You can know the language of faith and still resist the intimacy of God. Could it be that the Spirit is inviting you into a different kind of hearing—not the hurried hearing of a consumer, but the surrendered hearing of a disciple? Not "I heard that before," but "I will let that change me now."

When the Word Comes Alive — Revelation as frequency shift

Though often described as cold and logical, a computer's processing structure can echo certain aspects of human perception. At its most basic level, a machine operates through simple states—signal or silence, on or off. From these elementary conditions, extraordinary complexity emerges: images, memory, communication, learning. A programmer writes in higher languages—shaping raw operations into intelligible outcomes—yet beneath every elegant interface lies simplicity. Meaning is not in the data alone; it is in the framework that interprets it.

So it is with the Word of God. Scripture makes a sobering claim: a person may read sacred text and remain veiled. "Even unto this day, when Moses is read, the veil is upon their heart" (2 Corinthians 3:15). The text can be present while revelation is absent. Information may be available without transformation. And this is not merely a problem "out there." It is a temptation close to home. We can approach Scripture like a subject to master rather than a Voice to obey. We can learn its phrases without yielding to its Person. We can treat holy words as data instead of doorway.

Then comes the turning point: "Nevertheless when it shall turn to the Lord, the veil shall be taken away" (2 Corinthians 3:16). That is awakening. The Word does not change—but the listener does. Revelation arrives when the heart turns and the Spirit removes the veil. Suddenly the familiar becomes alive. The verse you have read a hundred times reads you. It exposes what you have hidden. It comforts what you have wounded. It names what you have avoided. Not because ink has power in itself, but because the Spirit who authored the Word now breathes upon it in your hearing.

Jesus names this plainly: "The words that I speak unto you, they are spirit, and they are life" (John 6:63). His Word is not merely instruction. It is impartation. Not merely sound. Life. And life does not remain external. Life enters. Life grows. Life rearranges the environment to make room for itself. The Word comes alive in you the way a seed comes alive in soil: quietly, patiently, insistently, pushing roots where you cannot see and bearing fruit where you could not manufacture it.

In the world of sound, a small shift in frequency can change everything. A note slightly detuned can make a whole chord feel uneasy. A receiver slightly off can turn music into static. You can be near the station and still not hear the song. But then, with one subtle adjustment, clarity returns. The receiver locks onto the signal. The noise falls away. The melody makes sense again. In that way, revelation can feel like a frequency shift—not because God changes His voice, but because the heart finally aligns with the voice that was there all along.

Interpretation implies intention. And intention implies an Author. You were not created merely to receive sound, but to recognize meaning. "In him we live, and move, and have our being" (Acts 17:28). Your capacity to awaken exists because you were formed within Him, not apart from Him. The hunger for truth is not proof you are empty; it is evidence you were designed for fullness. The ache itself is a kind of homing signal, calling you back toward the Source.

The Cost of Awakening — Why comfort often resists truth

Language carries authority. A word spoken becomes a path opened. A command released becomes a reality initiated. When God said, "Let there be light," the Word did not describe reality—it created it (Genesis 1:3). Creation emerged not from randomness, but from intentional speech ordered by divine will. That Word still speaks. But awakening to it is costly. Comfort prefers familiarity. Revelation disrupts it.

We often imagine awakening as a gentle sunrise—warmth spreading gradually, shadows lifting without resistance. And sometimes it is like that. But often it is more like the sudden turning on of a light in a room you have kept dim for a reason. You blink. You squint. You want to retreat. Because what is revealed is not only beauty; it is also disorder. It is dust in corners you pretended were clean. It is motives mixed with fear. It is grief you avoided by staying busy. Truth, when truly received, rearranges what you have protected.

Scripture does not soften this: "For the word of God is living and active, sharper than any two—edged sword... discerning the thoughts and intentions of the heart" (Hebrews 4:12). Awakening is not merely illuminating. It is exposing. The Word does not only comfort; it cuts. Not to harm, but to heal. A surgeon's scalpel is not cruelty; it is mercy. Yet mercy can still sting when it touches what has been infected.

This is why Jesus says, "If any man will come after me, let him deny himself, and take up his cross daily, and follow me" (Luke 9:23). Revelation does not arrive to decorate the self. It arrives to transform it. Many resist awakening not because truth is unclear, but because clarity requires surrender. It is one thing to admire God's holiness from a safe distance. It is another thing to let that holiness reach the hidden places where you have been managing your own survival—where you have been controlling outcomes, nursing resentment, postponing obedience, and calling it prudence.

Comfort resists truth because comfort often depends on illusion. We keep certain beliefs because they keep us safe, not because they are true. I cannot forgive because it would make what happened acceptable. I cannot trust because people always hurt me. I cannot slow down because everything will fall apart if I do. I cannot obey because I will lose what I love. These narratives can feel like protection. But over time they become a cage. Armor keeps out pain, yes, but it also keeps out love. And love is the very atmosphere in which awakening thrives.

Could it be that this is why people sometimes prefer religion over relationship? Religion can be managed. You can schedule it. You can measure it. You can perform it. Relationship cannot be controlled. Relationship reveals the authentic you and invites a response. It asks you to let love rearrange your priorities. And if the love is holy, it will not merely affirm you; it will sanctify you. Holiness is not the opposite of tenderness. Holiness is tenderness strong enough to make you whole.

Stillness as a Tuning Mechanism — Learning to quiet the noise

Not all influence arrives audibly. The human ear perceives only a narrow band of vibration within a vast field of unseen movement. Beneath and beyond our hearing exist frequencies that pass through us without our awareness. Yet the body listens. The nervous system entrains to pattern. The heart synchronizes with external signals. Some forms of reception occur beneath conscious awareness, long before words form. We are more porous than we think, and the world is always broadcasting.

Scripture has always framed this unseen activity spiritually: "For we wrestle not against flesh and blood, but against… spiritual wickedness in high places" (Ephesians 6:12). The unseen is not imaginary. It is active. And because it is active, stillness becomes essential. Stillness is not a luxury for the spiritually elite. It is a tuning mechanism for anyone who wants to hear clearly, a way of interrupting the constant broadcast of fear, accusation, and distraction that tries to occupy the inner room.

Elijah learned this when God bypassed the dramatic to speak through the quiet. The Lord was not in the wind, the earthquake, or the fire—but in a still, small voice (1 Kings 19:12). God can shake mountains, yet He chooses to whisper. Not because the whisper is timid, but because the whisper requires intimacy. A shout can be heard at a distance. A whisper demands closeness. A whisper invites you to come near.

"Be still and know that I am God" (Psalm 46:10). Stillness is a command, not a suggestion. And the fruit of stillness is knowing. There is an order Here that feels almost like spiritual physics: quiet alignment, then discernment. In a loud world, silence can feel like deprivation. We have grown accustomed to constant input—music, notifications, commentary, opinions. Silence can feel like being left alone with your own thoughts, and for many of us that is exactly what we fear. But stillness is not abandonment; it is the clearing of a space where God can be heard without competing noise.

If you have ever tried to tune an instrument, you know the first obstacle is not the string—it is the soundscape around it. When the environment is loud, it is hard to hear the subtle difference between sharp and flat. You can force the peg and hope you are close, but close is not the same as in tune. Sometimes you have to quiet the room. You have to listen carefully. You have to make small adjustments and listen again. In the same way, stillness is not spiritual laziness; it is spiritual precision. It is the humble practice of bringing your inner receiver into alignment with the voice of God.

Stillness also exposes the static we have normalized. In quiet, you begin to notice what has been governing you—anxieties you have called "responsibility," resentments you have called "wisdom," distractions you have called "rest." The Spirit is gentle, but He is not vague. In stillness He names things with love. He brings truth to the surface, not to shame you, but to free you. And freedom often sounds like clarity returning, like the inner receiver finally locking onto the station of peace.

Eyes to See, Ears to Hear — Awakening the whole being

"So then faith cometh by hearing, and hearing by the word of God" (Romans 10:17). Faith is not produced by effort, but by reception. The Word resonates before it convinces. It enters before it instructs. You can argue someone into agreement and still not awaken their soul. But the Spirit can whisper one sentence and shift an entire life. Faith is not a human achievement; it is a divine gift received through an open ear.

This is why Scripture repeatedly links awakening to perception: "He that hath ears to hear, let him hear" (Matthew 11:15). The issue is not sound, but readiness. And readiness is not merely mental. The whole being must awaken—not just the intellect. We are not brains collecting spiritual facts. We are embodied souls, designed to love, worship, obey, and become.

The Word of God is not aimed merely at your thoughts; it is aimed at your heart, your habits, your desires, and the reflexes you learned in pain.

Sound reveals what already exists but cannot yet be seen. In the womb, life is first disclosed through vibration before it is visible to the eye. What is hidden is revealed through resonance. A monitor translates tiny pulses into audible assurance: there is a heartbeat. There is a living presence that cannot yet be held but can be heard. In the same way, awakening often begins as resonance. You cannot yet "see" the full picture, but you can hear the heartbeat of truth. Something in you recognizes it, the way a child recognizes a mother's voice before fully understanding words.

Scripture names this reality: "While we look not at the things which are seen, but at the things which are not seen" (2 Corinthians 4:18). Awakening is the grace to perceive what has always been present. It is the Spirit opening the inner senses—the eyes of the heart, the ears of the soul. And then comes the heart of it all: "And the Word was made flesh and dwelt among us" (John 1:14). Heaven entered fully into human limitation. The divine Word stepped into time so what had fallen out of alignment could be restored from within.

Jesus lived in perfect synchronization with the Father: "The Son can do nothing of himself, but what He sees the Father do" (John 5:19). "As my Father hath taught me, I speak these things" (John 8:28). Father as Voice. Son as Word. Spirit as Breath. One God. One will. One harmony. In Jesus, the divine frequency became audible in human form. The eternal entered the temporal. The invisible became visible. The sound became flesh.

Awakening occurs when that resonance reaches us—not as concept, but as encounter. When the Word moves from page to presence. When hearing becomes knowing. When revelation becomes embodied. The Word became flesh so our flesh could receive the Word. He is still speaking. He is still calling. And when we truly listen, we are never the same.

So here you are, somewhere between information and revelation, somewhere between hearing and knowing. You may still have questions—honest, sincere, necessary questions. God is not threatened by them. But what if the deepest need beneath your questions is not more data, but more nearness? What if the Spirit is not trying to win your intellect, but to awaken your heart? There is a holy kindness in the way God calls. He does not shout you into submission. He draws you into surrender. He tunes you the way a master musician tunes a cherished instrument, not with impatience, but with intention—until the soul that once sounded like static begins to carry the clear, living resonance of the Voice that made it.

Awakening, then, is not an end but a beginning. It is the moment the soul realizes that life has always been unfolding in the presence of the Creator. What once felt distant now feels near. What once seemed ordinary now carries the quiet weight of wonder. The mind may still wrestle with questions, but the heart begins to recognize something deeper: the One who spoke the universe into existence is worthy not only of our curiosity, but of our reverence. And when that realization settles into the soul, awakening naturally turns into response—not driven by obligation, but by recognition. The heart begins to turn toward the One it now sees more clearly.

Spiritual awakening does not begin with understanding - it begins with a recognized response to the Truth.

Because once the soul recognizes the presence of God, neutrality becomes impossible. The only natural response is *worship*. Selah. (Wait here for a moment if you feel it.)

Enter Adoration.

ADORATION

When awakening opens our eyes to the presence of God, the Heart instinctively begins to respond. Throughout Scripture, the most common response to encountering the Creator is not analysis—it is worship. Men and women who suddenly recognize the nearness of God rarely begin with explanations; they begin with reverence. Something within the human soul recognizes the weight of holiness and turns toward it. Our hearts were designed for this reaction. Adoration is not merely a religious activity or a moment within a church service. It is the posture of a heart that has seen Him – if even just a glimpse - to know that He is worthy. And even so, we respond!

The Selah you entered was not a pause in the narrative—it was a passage into sacred space. Not a room you built with effort, but a threshold you crossed by surrender. You did not "achieve" it. You consented to it. You stopped reaching for the next thought long enough to notice the One who has been there the whole time.

What is occurring is not an exercise. It is an invitation.

Invitation implies Personhood. It assumes the universe is not merely a system to decode but a Presence to encounter. It suggests that the Holy One is not hiding behind the mechanics of life like a distant engineer but drawing near like a Father who wants to be known. "Draw near to God, and He will draw near to you" (James 4:8). That is not the language of a deity who must be earned. It is the language of a God who responds to humility with nearness.

Adoration restores perspective. It helps the reader see that worship reorders the soul.

Worship is the human soul coming into right proportion with its Creator.

Could it be that the first miracle in any season of awakening is not what we discover, but what we finally allow? The unclenching. The release of the inner manager. The quiet admission that God cannot be reduced to the dimensions of our need. When Moses asked for God's name, the answer did not fit inside a label: "I AM WHO I AM" (Exodus 3:14). Not a tool. Not a concept. Not an accessory to our goals. I AM.

In that Selah, you may have sensed a holy paradox: God was immense, and God was near. Scripture holds both without apology. The seraphim cry, "Holy, holy, holy is the LORD of hosts" (Isaiah 6:3), and yet the psalmist can say, "The LORD is near to all who call on Him" (Psalm 145:18). Otherness and intimacy. Transcendence and tenderness. If we are honest, part of us wants one without the other: nearness without awe, or awe without vulnerability. But adoration keeps them married. It allows God to remain holy without becoming distant, and near without becoming familiar in the cheap sense of the word.

This is the heart of adoration.

Adoration is worship without agenda. It is the decision to come near without asking God to perform. No transaction. No negotiation. No subtle attempt to steer the moment toward a desired outcome. Just presence—mutual, reverent, and deeply personal. Not casual, but close. Not careless, but consecrated. It is like stepping into a cathedral where you cannot control the echo; you can only hear it. Or like standing at the edge of a dark ocean: you do not command the tide, and yet it reaches for your feet.

Worship aligns the human heart because it restores proper orientation between the Creator and the created. Much of human struggle comes from misalignment—when our attention, affection, and identity become centered on things that were never meant to carry that weight. When we worship, our focus shifts away from ourselves and back toward God. In that shift, perspective begins to correct itself. The soul remembers who God is and who we are in relation to Him.

Scripture consistently shows that what we behold shapes what we become. Worship places our attention on the holiness, goodness, and authority of God. As the heart lingers there, something subtle begins to change. The mind quiets. Pride softens. Fear loosens its grip. The soul begins to recalibrate, much like an instrument being tuned to the correct pitch.

This is why worship has always been central to the life of faith. It is not merely an expression of devotion—it is a form of alignment. When the human heart fixes its attention on God, the disorder within us begins to settle. Our desires, priorities, and perceptions gradually come back into harmony with the One who created us.

In that sense, worship is not simply something we give to God. It is also something God uses to restore us. The more clearly we behold Him, the more the soul begins to resonate with His character. And in that resonance, the human heart finds the alignment it was created for.

Adoration as Alignment

Adoration is not merely an expression; it is alignment. Worship restores orientation the way a compass needle settles when you stop shaking it. You do not force north into existence. You simply let the needle come to rest.

Jesus taught His disciples to pray with this kind of re—centering. Before requests, before daily bread, before deliverance from temptation, the prayer begins with reverence: "Our Father in Heaven, hallowed be Your name" (Matthew 6:9). The heart is turned Godward first. Because what is wrong in us is not only what we lack; it is what we are oriented toward. Adoration reorders the inner world. It dethrones the self without humiliating the self. It quietly places God back where He belongs.

If these chapters have been speaking in the language of signal and reception, then adoration is the moment the receiver turns toward the

Source. In communication theory, a message's fidelity depends not only on the transmitter, but on the channel and the receiver—on noise, distortion, bandwidth, and alignment (Claude Shannon, 1948). Spiritually, God is not the fragile part of the system. "God is not a man, that He should lie" (Numbers 23:19). He is faithful. He speaks. He acts. He remains. The question is whether we are aligned enough to receive what is being given.

Noise, in signal processing, is not always the obvious roar. Sometimes it is a baseline hum—a "noise floor" that limits what can be detected (Oppenheim & Schafer, 2010). Many souls live with an elevated noise floor: constant evaluation, constant self—protection, constant hurry. Even in prayer, we may be scanning for results, measuring whether we "felt" something, judging the moment as successful or not. That internal commentary becomes static. God can whisper and we can miss Him—not because He is silent, but because we are loud.

It does not do so by force, but by reverence. When you bow, you stop competing with God for center stage. When you adore, you stop narrating your own performance. You become present. "Be still and know that I am God" (Psalm 46:10). **Stillness is not emptiness; it is attention. It is the kind of silence that is actually a yes.**

And because humans are integrated creatures, that yes is not only spiritual; it is embodied. Scripture repeatedly joins inner reverence with outward posture—kneeling, lifting hands, falling facedown (Psalm 95:6; 1 Kings 8:54; Revelation 7:11). Not because God needs choreography, but because the body often leads the heart back into truth. Contemporary cognitive science describes "embodied cognition"—the way bodily states and actions shape perception and meaning—making (Lakoff & Johnson, 1999; Barsalou, 2008). When the body stops performing and begins to yield, the heart often follows.

Something else happens, too, beneath conscious thought. The nervous system that has learned to brace—against rejection, against disappointment, against the next unpredictable turn—begins to soften. Modern models of autonomic regulation describe how states of safety and connection support openness, learning, and relational attunement (Porges, 2011). We do not need to spiritualize physiology to see the mercy in it: when the body feels safe, the heart becomes more capable of trust. Could it be that worship becomes a sanctuary not only for the soul, but for the whole person God formed?

Yet adoration is not merely calm. It is consecration. Peace is not the goal; God is. Sometimes adoration steadies us, and sometimes it undoes us. Isaiah worshiped and then cried out, "Woe is me!" (Isaiah 6:5). Peter encountered Jesus and fell at His knees, saying, "Depart from me, for I am a sinful man, O Lord" (Luke 5:8). In both cases, the encounter was not manipulation; it was revelation. The presence of holiness exposes what is out of order, and exposure is not cruelty—it is cure.

Worship is the great recalibrator because it restores truth in the deepest place: the place where we decide who is worthy of our trust.

Scripture uses embodied language because worship is not merely an idea; it is a posture. The primary New Testament verb often translated "to worship," proskuneō (προσκυνέω), describes bowing low in homage—falling down before One deemed worthy (Matthew 2:11; John 4:24). Lexicons emphasize the sense of prostration and reverent submission (BDAG, 3rd ed.; LSJ). Many teachers also note the ancient gesture implied by the word—devotion expressed as "kissing toward" in acts of homage. Whether the emphasis lands on knees, lips, or the lowered self, the meaning is the same: worship is a yielded life.

The Old Testament carries similar weight. "Oh come, let us worship and bow down; let us kneel before the LORD, our Maker!" (Psalm 95:6). And Psalm 2 summons allegiance with striking imagery: "Kiss the Son" (Psalm 2:12). The Hebrew phrase is richly discussed, yet the movement of the psalm is clear: reverence, allegiance, refuge (Psalm 2:11–12; HALOT). This is not devotion demanded at sword point. It is devotion offered because reality has been recognized. The rightful King is not made King by our worship; He is recognized as King through it.

This is what adoration restores: right order.

And right order matters more than we realize, because spiritual pursuit can fracture at the moment it becomes useful. The drift is rarely dramatic. It is often sincere. We enter God's presence because we need Him, and need is not shameful. "Cast all your anxieties on Him, because He cares for you" (1 Peter 5:7). Yet somewhere along the way, we may begin to treat His presence as a means rather than a meeting. Some call it seeking His hand instead of His face. Worship becomes a tool for calming, a method for manifesting, an atmosphere for generating a spiritual outcome. We begin to approach God with an invisible contract. If I do this, then You will do that. If I sing long enough, if I pray hard enough, if I become holy enough, then You will answer in the way I have imagined.

Could it be that the most subtle form of idolatry is not loving the wrong god, but using the right God?

When worship shifts from adoration to utility, revelation becomes extraction. We no longer receive what God gives; we attempt to pull what we want. And extraction always leaves the soul hungry, because what we were designed for is not merely a change in circumstance, but communion with the Living One. "This is eternal life, that they know You, the only true God, and Jesus Christ whom You have sent" (John 17:3). Knowing. Not managing. Not harnessing. Knowing.

The Temptation to Self—Activate

Here is where the line begins to appear, the quiet boundary that spiritual pursuit must honor. Awakening that begins in reverence can turn inward when pride is allowed to take root. The moment awareness becomes self—referential rather than God—directed, perception distorts. What was meant to deepen dependence becomes a platform for self—elevation. Scripture names this drift without flinching: "God opposes the proud but gives grace to the humble" (James 4:6; 1 Peter 5:5).

Pride is not merely an attitude; it is a posture. It is the refusal to live as dependent. And it can wear religious clothing. It can take the form of secret superiority—believing you see more than others, know more than others, have "gone deeper" than others. It can even take the form of spiritual impatience: I have waited long enough; I deserve results. In that moment, the heart begins to self—activate.

Self—activation is the belief that understanding grants authority. That insight authorizes action. That knowledge justifies autonomy. Revelation becomes permission. Yet Scripture never equates knowing with governing. Wisdom is offered, but it is offered within reverence: "The fear of the LORD is the beginning of wisdom" (Proverbs 9:10). And "Trust in the LORD with all your heart, and do not lean on your own understanding" (Proverbs 3:5). Understanding is not demonized; it is dethroned.

The pattern is ancient. In Eden, the seduction was not merely disobedience, but autonomous discernment—"You will be like God, knowing good and evil" (Genesis 3:5). The allure was godlikeness without God. And the consequence was not freedom but hiding (Genesis 3:8–10). The signal broke, not because God stopped speaking, but because the receiver turned away.

Self—activation feels empowering, but it quietly removes God from the center. It exchanges listening for asserting, responding for initiating, worship for control. And once that exchange occurs, the spiritual life becomes a project. Projects require managers. The self volunteers for the job. God becomes an assistant, a consultant, a backup plan.

Alchemy: Power Without Permission

This is how adoration can slip toward alchemy.

Spiritual alchemy rarely begins through overt darkness. It often begins through longing—the desire to heal, to awaken, to become whole. Desire itself is not wrong. "As a deer pants for flowing streams, so pants my soul for You, O God" (Psalm 42:1). Longing can be a homing signal. But longing becomes dangerous when it becomes desperate, because desperation will take any door that looks like relief.

Historically, alchemy sought transformation through manipulation and technique, attempting to turn base matter into something higher or more powerful (Principe, 2013). The modern spiritual version borrows that impulse: change achieved through inner mastery, secret knowledge, or methods that promise power without surrender. God may still be named, but He is no longer central. The self becomes the altar, the priest, and the reward.

Spiritual alchemy promises illumination without obedience, healing without holiness, transformation without dependence. It offers a counterfeit exchange that feels empowering because it loops inward. And in systems language, loops can become unstable. In audio engineering, a microphone too close to a speaker produces feedback—sound amplifying itself until it overwhelms the room. In control theory, unchecked positive feedback can drive a system toward instability (Ogata, 2010). The system is not transmitting a new song; it is amplifying itself.

It is entirely possible to experience heightened awareness, emotional release, even moments of clarity—without ever encountering the living God. That is illumination without revelation. Scripture's revelation is relational: "No one knows the Father except the Son and anyone to whom the Son chooses to reveal Him" (Matthew 11:27). **Revelation is not extracted by cleverness. It is received in relationship**. That is why Jesus' invitation is not "unlock the hidden laws," but "Follow Me" (Matthew 4:19). Not "master the method," but "abide" (John 15:4).

One of the most subtle dangers of our time is how easily we can live off of someone else's revelation without ever receiving our own from the Source.

We have unprecedented access—sermons on demand, clips from our favorite preachers, endless streams of "words of the Lord" that inspire, motivate, and move us emotionally. And while these can be good, even helpful, they were never meant to replace personal encounter.

Because borrowed revelation has a limit.

If what you are receiving is not becoming *your* revelation—personally revealed, personally wrestled with, personally received—you are, in effect, short-circuiting the signal. You may feel energized for a moment, but over time, something begins to fade.

And eventually, you burn out.

Not because the truth wasn't real—but because it was never rooted in you.

God's voice was never meant to be secondhand. It is living, personal, and present. What He speaks to another can point you in the right direction—but it cannot replace what He desires to speak directly to you.

Lucifer's Error

Pride is misaligned brilliance.

Isaiah's prophetic poetry gives language to an ancient spiritual posture: "You said in your heart, 'I will ascend to Heaven… I will make myself like the Most High'" (Isaiah 14:13–14). The passage has historical layers, yet the spiritual principle is consistent across Scripture: the enemy's impulse is self—exaltation against God (cf. Ezekiel 28:17; Luke 10:18).

The fall is not born of ignorance, but of re—centering—shifting from reflection to replacement, from worship to self—regard.

The strategy has not changed. The temptation is not always overt evil; it is autonomy. It is the whisper that you can become whole without submission, awakened without worship, powerful without permission. It is the promise of being "like God" without being with God (Genesis 3:5).

Why God Withholds Power Until Posture Is Right

Here is a mercy we often misunderstand: God does not withhold power as punishment. He withholds it as protection.

We equate power with maturity, but Scripture often equates maturity with humility. Moses is called "very meek" (Numbers 12:3). David is anointed and then hidden (1 Samuel 16:12–13). Jesus Himself lived under the Father's will, saying, "The Son can do nothing of His own accord, but only what He sees the Father doing" (John 5:19). And He tells us plainly, "Apart from Me you can do nothing" (John 15:5). This is not limitation for limitation's sake. It is design. Life in God is dependent participation.

Humility, then, is not weakness. It is truth—alignment. "God opposes the proud but gives grace to the humble" (James 4:6). Grace is not only forgiveness; it is power that does not corrupt because it is carried in surrender. Pride does not merely offend God; it distorts reception. It bends everything inward. Humility restores clarity.

And the language of resonance helps us feel why. In physics and acoustics, resonance is the amplified response that occurs when a system is driven near its natural frequency (Halliday, Resnick, & Walker, 2014). Resonance is powerful, but it is not neutral. It magnifies whatever the system already is. If the structure is sound, resonance can create beauty—an instrument singing, a room warming with harmonics. If the structure is compromised, resonance can be destructive—amplifying weakness until fracture occurs.

Could it be that God waits for posture because He refuses to amplify what would destroy us?

Jesus warns that activity can exist without intimacy: "Many will say to Me… 'Did we not do many mighty works in Your name?'… and then will I declare to them, 'I never knew you'" (Matthew 7:22–23). The issue is not that God hates power. The issue is that power without relationship is a counterfeit kingdom. The aim of God is not to make us impressive; it is to make us like His Son (Romans 8:29). That likeness is formed in surrender.

All revelation beyond this point will remain incomplete unless it flows through Jesus Christ, "the way, and the truth, and the life" (John 14:6). He is not merely a figure in history; He is the Word through whom all things were made (John 1:1–3), the One in whom all things hold together (Colossians 1:17). If we are speaking in the language of frequency, He is not a technique within the system. He is the Source. To bypass Him is to study sound without hearing. It is to chase light without seeing.

And this is why "faith" matters so deeply. "Without faith it is impossible to please Him, for whoever would draw near to God must believe that He exists and that He rewards those who seek Him" (Hebrews 11:6). Faith is not mental gymnastics; it is relational openness. It is the posture that keeps the receiver pointed toward the Source. Faith says, "Speak, LORD, for Your servant hears" (1 Samuel 3:10). Faith refuses to self—activate. Faith waits to be led.

"When the Spirit of truth comes, He will guide you into all the truth" (John 16:13). Guidance implies movement and surrender. Truth is not merely a conclusion; it is a path walked with a Person.

So let this chapter become a gentle checkpoint in your pursuit. Not a warning meant to shrink you, but a mercy meant to keep you whole. Whenever your seeking begins to feel like control, return. Whenever your curiosity begins to crave power, return. Whenever your worship begins to carry an agenda, return. Come back to adoration—the place where God is beheld, not used; where presence is prized above outcome; where you kneel without leverage and discover that His nearness is not purchased by technique, but received by humility.

And as you linger there, something quiet will keep happening. The soul will re—order. The noise will lower. The heart will soften. Not because you learned the secret, but because you met the Holy One. Perhaps that is the truest transformation: not the power to transmute life through hidden knowledge, but the grace to be changed by Love Himself (1 John 4:8–10), until your pursuit becomes what it was always meant to be—communion with God, and the joy of finally being aligned.

The Veil Torn – Reverence Made Near

In the Old Testament, nearness to God was never casual. It was not that God was cold; it was that God was holy. The God who walked in the garden with humanity (Genesis 3:8) was the same God whose glory made Sinai tremble (Exodus 19:16–20). When He drew near, reality behaved differently. Fire, cloud, boundary lines, priests, blood, incense—Scripture is almost relentless in its insistence that the living God is not to be approached the way we approach everything else.

There is a sobriety woven into the Old Covenant that we modern readers can misunderstand. We often read those moments of "severity" as evidence of harshness, when they may actually be the evidence of truth: that holiness is not a metaphor. Nadab and Abihu treat the sacred casually and are consumed (Leviticus 10:1–3). Uzzah reaches toward the ark as if the holy can be stabilized by human instinct and he falls dead (2 Samuel 6:6–7). Even Moses, the friend of God, is told, "You cannot see My face, for man shall not see Me and live" (Exodus 33:20). And when

Isaiah, a prophet, encounters the unveiled throne room, his first response is not confidence but collapse: "Woe is me… for my eyes have seen the King" (Isaiah 6:5).

So yes—reverence was demanded, and familiarity could become contempt. But notice what that "contempt" often is: it is not intimacy; it is presumption. Reverence and nearness are not opposites in Scripture. Presumption and holiness are.

The problem is that sinful humanity cannot maintain nearness without distortion. Under the Old Covenant, the system was protective. It taught Israel that God is not an object to handle. It instructed the people in the weight of glory. It built boundaries not because God disliked them, but because He loved them enough not to let them come near unprepared. "You cannot… and live" was not an insult; it was an honest description of what happens when fallen humanity collides with unmediated holiness.

And yet, if we read carefully, we also see God's ache for nearness threaded through that same Old Testament. He "walked" with His people by pillar and cloud (Exodus 13:21–22). He placed His name in their midst (Deuteronomy 12:11). He allowed a tabernacle—an outrageous idea—so that the Holy One could "dwell among" them (Exodus 25:8). Even the reverence of the law was, in part, a tutoring: teaching the human heart how to approach without being consumed.

Which brings us to a valid question—why did Jesus come to fulfill the law?

Because the law wasn't merely a list. It was a covenantal architecture designed to do at least three things at once: reveal God's holiness, reveal humanity's condition, and provide a temporary way for a holy God to remain with an unholy people without destroying them. Paul says, "Through the law comes knowledge of sin" (Romans 3:20). The law exposes what we are, not to shame us, but to show us that the problem is deeper than behavior—it is a nature. And once the problem is named, the heart starts to long for a solution that reaches deeper than self—improvement.

Jesus fulfills the law because the law was never the destination. It was the road that leads to the Person. "Do not think that I have come to abolish the Law or the Prophets; I have not come to abolish them but to fulfill them" (Matthew 5:17). Fulfillment implies completion, not cancellation. The law's sacrificial system pointed forward to a true sacrifice (Hebrews 10:1–10). The priesthood pointed forward to a true mediator (Hebrews 7:23–28). The temple pointed forward to God dwelling with man in a new way (John 1:14; Revelation 21:3). The holiness codes pointed forward to a holy people transformed from the inside out (Jeremiah 31:31–34; Hebrews 8:8–12).

Jesus fulfills the law because God's goal was never to keep humanity at a safe distance forever. The goal was to bring humanity near *without losing holiness.* That's the miracle. Not that God decided to become less holy so we could feel comfortable, but that He made a way for us to become truly clean so we could draw near.

This is where the story becomes personal to all of us.

Because the longing you described—the need for nearness, the ache to be loved, the instinct to seek approval through connection—that longing is not random. It is a fingerprint. We were made for communion. We were built with an interior space that only the Creator can fill without cracking the structure. Augustine famously prayed, "Our hearts are restless until they rest in You." And Scripture echoes that restlessness in different words: "As a deer pants for flowing streams, so pants my soul for You, O God" (Psalm 42:1). That thirst isn't merely emotional; it's theological. It is the soul remembering its intended atmosphere.

Yet that same longing can become the engine of idolatry if it is aimed at the wrong source. We will ask people to be gods for us. We will ask careers to be saviors. We will ask admiration to be identity. We will ask romance to be redemption. And when they fail—because they must fail—we are tempted to harden. We become cynical, self—protective, numb. Not because we are evil, but because we are wounded and tired of hoping.

And into that tiredness, the gospel speaks like a door opening.

Jesus did not fulfill the law so we could stop revering God. He fulfilled the law so we could stop being separated from God. He did not come to erase holiness; He came to make holiness *habitable.* He came to do in His own body what the law could only symbolize—deal with sin at its root, cleanse the conscience, and bring us near.

This is why the New Testament speaks with such daring language. "We have confidence to enter the holy places by the blood of Jesus" (Hebrews 10:19). Confidence—not arrogance. Nearness—not presumption. "Let us then with confidence draw near to the throne of grace" (Hebrews 4:16). The throne is still a throne—God is still God—but it is called "grace" because the One seated there has made a way for you to come.

The moment the veil tore at Jesus' crucifixion (Matthew 27:51), the universe was preaching. The barrier between God and man—symbolized by the temple curtain—was being ripped open by the act of atonement. It was as if God Himself was saying: the distance is over. Not because I have lowered My standards, but because My Son has carried your separation and ended it.

And that is the tender answer to your line: He would rather have a relationship of nearness with us than to be revered from afar.

But notice the shape of that nearness. It is not nearness that trivializes God; it is nearness purchased at great cost. It is nearness that transforms us. In Christ, you are not invited into a casual acquaintance with the Divine. You are invited into adoption. "To all who did receive Him...

He gave the right to become children of God" (John 1:12). Children do not approach their father like an employee approaches a boss. Yet a healthy child does not despise a good father either. The child runs in with trust because love has removed fear—but the father's strength remains.

Perhaps that is what it means to be made in His image: not merely that we long to be loved, but that we are designed to love in return. We are relational beings because God is relational. We are built for communion because God is communion within Himself—Father, Son, Spirit (Matthew 28:19). And the gospel is not God granting us a spiritual technique; it is God granting us Himself.

So the question becomes exactly what you wrote: will we realize His call to us? Can we answer with sincerity?

Sincerity is not perfection. Sincerity is openness. It is the willingness to be addressed. It is the refusal to hide behind spiritual performance or intellectual distance. It is the quiet trembling yes of Samuel: "Speak, LORD, for Your servant hears" (1 Samuel 3:10). It is the honest prayer of the father in the crowd: "I believe; help my unbelief!" (Mark 9:24). It is the simplest turning of the heart toward the light.

And then that urgent line lands with fresh weight: "Today, if you hear His voice, do not harden your hearts" (Psalm 95:7–8; quoted in Hebrews 3:7–8; Hebrews 4:7).

Hardened hearts are not usually forged in one dramatic decision. They are formed by small refusals—by repeated delays, by protecting ourselves from disappointment, by treating God as an idea rather than a Person. Soft hearts are formed the same way: by repeated yeses, by choosing to come near again, by letting reverence become intimacy instead of distance.

So perhaps the invitation is not to choose between reverence and nearness at all. Perhaps the invitation is to let Jesus make them one—so that your nearness is reverent, and your reverence is near. Not adored from afar like a star you can admire but never touch, and not handled like a tool you can use, but encountered as He is: holy and close, blazing and gentle, King and Father. You've heard that its His kindness that lead

And if the gospel is true, then this moment—this "today"—is not random. It is the sound of God calling you by name, not to pressure you, but to bring you home. Lovingly, the Father calls to you—not to demand, but to draw. In this moment, His perfect love casts out fear (I John 4:18), and the distorted view of Him begins to melt away. You choose surrender. You trust the still small Voice. And something shifts.

This is the sacred threshold where humility births pliability—and pliability gives way to true alignment. The heart begins to resonate with the One it was created to know. And when that resonance deepens, worship becomes something more than reverence.

When the heart truly beholds God, worship becomes alignment.

Enter your Alignment.

ALIGNMENT

Every step of this journey has been leading to this moment. From the Voice that spoke creation into existence, to the Architect who designed it, to the breath given to humanity, to the patterns through which God forms His people, and the awakening that stirs the heart toward worship—each movement leads toward a singular posture: alignment. Here, the threads of sound, science, and Scripture converge. **Alignment is where the Sound of God becomes more than an idea; it becomes the ordering center of a human life. It is the moment when the soul stops merely observing the Creator's work and begins to resonate with His voice.** When that resonance takes hold, faith is no longer something we simply believe—it has become substance; it becomes something we live.

Why Humanity Drifts

Humanity rarely drifts because it consciously rejects God. More often, we drift because our attention becomes divided. From the beginning, the human heart has been surrounded by competing voices—fear, ambition, insecurity, cultural expectations, and the quiet pressure to define ourselves apart from the Creator. Over time, those voices begin to shape our thoughts and desires. What once felt clear becomes blurred. What once felt centered becomes scattered. Drift happens gradually, almost imperceptibly, as the soul begins to orient itself around something other than the One who gave it life.

Scripture describes this condition in many ways—wandering, forgetting, hardening of the heart—but the underlying reality is the same: the human soul loses its reference point. Like an instrument slowly slipping out of tune, we begin to resonate with the wrong frequencies. Our priorities shift. Our desires misfire. Our sense of identity becomes unstable. Not because we were created for chaos, but because we were created for alignment and have forgotten the voice that set our design in motion.

Alignment, then, is not about forcing ourselves into spiritual performance. It is about returning—recalibrating the heart to the voice that has been calling us all along.

What Alignment Actually Is — Not effort, but agreement

There is a particular kind of tension that settles into the human heart when the evidence of the Divine begins to feel too weighty to dismiss, and yet too holy to reduce. And that recognition is unsettling in the most sacred way, because it presses on the place where we like to be safe. We want a world that can be explained. We want a God who can be summarized. We want to keep the holy at arm's length, as long as we can still claim we believe. But the moment you begin to suspect the message is personal, you are forced into a threshold decision. If God is real and speaking, then neutrality is not a resting place. You can pretend it is, but you will feel the strain. The soul was not designed to hover forever in the doorway.

Faith lives in that doorway. Not as fragile optimism, not as religious aesthetic, not as a mental trick for coping with pain, but as a way of receiving what cannot be contained by the senses alone. Scripture does not treat faith as poetic filler. It names faith as substance. "Faith is the substance of things hoped for, the evidence of things not seen" (Hebrews 11:1). Substance is a word with weight. Evidence is a word with gravity. Both belong to the language of reality, not fantasy.

And yet the reality faith perceives is not the kind that submits to being controlled.

This is where modern minds often stumble—not because they are incapable of belief, but because they are trained to treat measurement as the gatekeeper of what is real. If it can be quantified, it is credible. If it cannot, it is suspicious. But what if measurement is not the gatekeeper of reality, only one tool of interaction? What if our insistence on "proof" is sometimes less about truth and more about control? Because proof, when demanded as a condition of trust, becomes a subtle attempt to remain sovereign over the encounter.

But God—if He is God—will not be made a subject beneath our microscope.

We do not come to Him as investigators examining an object. We come to Him as creatures approaching a Creator, as children approaching a Father, as those who have been spoken into existence now turning toward the Voice. "Without faith it is impossible to please Him, for He who comes to God must believe that He is, and that He is a rewarder of those who diligently seek Him" (Hebrews 11:6). Notice how that verse carries both tenderness and steel. Faith is not an accessory; it is the posture of approach. To come to God is to come believing He is—and believing that He responds to seekers.

This is where alignment becomes necessary.

Because if faith is agreement with God's reality, then alignment is the posture that makes that agreement possible—not once, but continually. Alignment is not primarily moral performance, though it will shape morality. It is not primarily emotional intensity, though it will affect feeling. It is not primarily intellectual assent, though it will transform understanding. Alignment is first relational return—an inward reorientation that says, You are God. I am not. You are the source. I am the receiver. You are the origin. I am the echo. That is not humiliation. It is reality. And reality, when embraced, is freedom.

The world may call faith wishful thinking. Scripture treats faith as reception. It keeps returning to verbs of perception and response: hearing, seeing, tasting, knowing, discerning. "Taste and see that the Lord is good" (Psalm 34:8). "My sheep hear My voice, and I know them, and they follow Me" (John 10:27). "He who has ears to hear, let him hear" (Mark 4:9; Matthew 11:15; Revelation 2:7). God speaks as though connection is normal—because it is.

Misalignment is the interruption, not the design.

This is why the language of alignment matters. Not because we are trying to turn spirituality into science, but because the world God made is full of metaphors that refuse to stay merely metaphorical. We learn about our own hearts through the way creation behaves. We learn about reception through the way sound behaves.

We learn about drift through the way instruments behave. We learn about clarity through the way signals behave. And if we are honest, most of us know what misalignment feels like long before we know how to name it. It feels like static. Like spiritual fuzz. Like you can't quite hear, can't quite settle, can't quite rest. You are doing the right things, but something is off.

It is tempting in those moments to blame God for not speaking clearly. But what if the issue is not His clarity? What if the issue is my posture? What if I am near the station but not tuned?

The broadcast is faithful; the receiver needs tuning.

This is where many believers get stuck. We assume alignment means trying harder—doing better, cleaning up, staying consistent, proving sincerity. We assume it is primarily moral exertion: if I behave well enough, I will finally "deserve" clarity. But alignment is not first about effort. Alignment is agreement. It is the inner "yes" that turns the whole being back toward God—posture before productivity, surrender before striving.

The remedy is not more effort. It is recalibration.

And recalibration sounds gentle until you realize what it requires. It requires confession. It requires humility. It requires stillness. It requires the surrender of the illusion that you can keep running the show while also receiving the peace of a surrendered life. It requires you to admit that you can be sincere and still be misaligned. You can love God and still be living from fear. You can worship on Sunday and still be ruled by control on Monday. You can know Scripture and still be withholding your heart.

Alignment is not religious strain. Alignment is relational return.

At some point in my own life, God began to show me the difference between being informed about Him and being aligned with Him. I had learned the language. I had heard sermons. I could recognize the vocabulary of faith. But there were moments—quiet ones, sometimes painful ones—when I realized I was listening to God like a person listening to music through a wall: I could tell something was playing, but I couldn't make out the melody. I could sense Presence but not always find the message. And in those moments, I wanted something I could control: a method, a formula, a guarantee.

But God did not offer me control. He offered me Himself.

And in His mercy, He began to give me images that didn't reduce Him but did help me bow. He gave me language for the unseen shaping the seen. He gave me metaphors that carried enough precision to steady my mind, and enough mystery to keep me reverent.

One day, while preparing to teach about sound, I encountered the concept of cymatics—visual patterns formed when sound vibration interacts with matter. I watched particles gather into symmetrical shapes as frequencies changed. I watched order emerge from the invisible. My mind was fascinated, but my spirit was moved in a different way. It didn't feel like proof. It felt like a parable. It was as if God was whispering, See? The unseen is not empty. It is active. It forms. It shapes. It sustains. It was beckoning of sorts to trust what I could not see. Even when it meant not making sense or understanding it.

And I remember thinking—could it be that faith opens the door to the unseen? And what lies beyond that door is so much bigger than my imagination? Could it be that faith is the act of aligning with what is already true, even when my senses cannot fully verify it? Could it be that the spiritual realm is not a mystical place that seems to mesmerize and hold us in contempt with fear? Maybe it a real space that simply lies beyond the bandwidth my natural senses were designed to carry?

Not beyond my spirit, though.

Understanding that creation responds—and that God "upholds all things by the word of His power" (Hebrews 1:3)—began to reframe the way I saw Him. Not as distant or abstract, but present, sustaining, and continually expressing Himself through what He has made (Psalm 19:1). It helped me grasp that faith might be less about belief without evidence and more about tuning into a deeper frequency—one that aligns us with the Creator's voice moving through all things: in us, around us, and through us.

But we must be careful here. The point is not to suggest that God can be reduced to a mechanism. He remains outside the scope of human proof. He is not a specimen. He is the Source. The scientific parallels are not meant to contain Him; they are meant to awaken wonder in the mind so the heart can bow. They affirm design. They invite reverence. They help us perceive that the world is not as closed as our cynicism insists.

Faith is not the product of our imagination. Faith is the posture that says, If God is real and speaking, I will lean in until I can discern Him. When that resonance takes hold, faith is no longer something we reach for in uncertainty—it becomes substance, shaping the life we live. And this is why Scripture keeps returning to language—like hearing. "Faith comes by hearing, and hearing by the Word of God" (Romans 10:17). Hearing is not mere exposure. It is reception. It is internalization. It is yielding. It is agreement with Christ Himself, the Word.

This is why people can sit through sermons every week and remain unchanged. They heard words, but they did not hear God. They received information, but they did not receive transformation. Because the Word of God is more than text on a page meant to inform the mind. The Word of God is God's voice speaking—sometimes through Scripture, sometimes through conviction, sometimes through direction that calls us into repentance and obedience.

Not as punishment. As posture.

Obedience is not the price we pay to earn connection; it is the fruit of connection. It is what happens when the heart is aligned enough to recognize the Voice and respond. "If you love Me, keep My commandments" (John 14:15). Love comes first. Relationship comes first. Hearing comes first. And from that place, obedience becomes less like strain and more like resonance.

So alignment, at its simplest, is relational return. It is agreement. It is the whole being turning toward God, not partially, not occasionally, not privately, but wholly.

Spirit, Soul, and Body in Harmony — Whole—being faith

If alignment is agreement, the next question becomes painfully practical. What part of me is agreeing?

Most believers do not struggle with believing God exists. They struggle with believing Him with their whole being. They struggle with coherence. They struggle with being gathered rather than divided.

We treat faith like a single switch. On or off. Strong or weak. Present or absent. But Scripture does not describe faith as a disconnected idea floating inside us. Scripture describes a person being brought back into wholeness. Paul prays, "May the God of peace Himself sanctify you completely; and may your whole spirit, soul, and body be preserved blameless" (1 Thessalonians 5:23). Completely. Whole. Spirit, soul, and body. God is not after a piece of you. He is after you.

Your spirit is the part of you designed for God. It is where communion happens—where the Holy Spirit convicts, comforts, corrects, and leads. Jesus speaks of worship "in spirit and truth" (John 4:24). Not truth without spirit. Not spirit without truth. Both. Alignment begins when your spirit turns toward Him, not as an idea, but as a Person.

When your spirit is aligned, there is a kind of inner clarity that does not depend on outward ease. You may still have grief. You may still have questions. You may still face storms. But deep inside, the center is facing Him. The receiver is pointed toward the Source.

But the soul is where many believers become conflicted. The soul is the realm of mind, will, emotions, memory, and interpretation—the stories we tell ourselves about what life means, what pain means, what God is like, who we are, what we must do to be safe. The soul is where old scripts run. It is where trauma echoes. It is where fear rehearses. It is where shame hides.

This is why Scripture places such emphasis on renewal: "Be transformed by the renewing of your mind" (Romans 12:2). Renewal is alignment at the level of interpretation. A person can be spiritually hungry and still mentally chaotic. A person can love God and still believe lies about God. A person can pray and still be ruled by fear because the mind is running an old narrative.

Alignment is not pretending those narratives aren't there. Alignment is bringing them into God's presence until they begin to submit to truth. It is allowing the Word of God to rewrite the inner story. It is allowing the Spirit of God to heal the places that have been driving your reactions from underneath.

"Keep your heart with all diligence, for out of it spring the issues of life" (Proverbs 4:23). The inner life doesn't stay inner. It leaks. It shapes your speech, your relationships, your decisions, and your body. It is why people can say, "I trust God," while living in anxiety. It is why we can confess, "God is good," while bracing for abandonment. It is why we can quote Scripture while staying trapped in the same responses.

The spirit may be turned toward God, but the soul may still be broadcasting static.

And then there is the body.

The body is not separate from spiritual life. It is the place where inner agreements become physical habits. It is where obedience becomes visible. It is where stress shows up. It is where peace is felt. It is where worship is expressed. Scripture does not treat the body as irrelevant. "Present your bodies a living sacrifice" (Romans 12:1). "Your body is a temple of the Holy Spirit" (1 Corinthians 6:19). The body is not a nuisance to spiritual life; it is a participant.

So when we talk about alignment, we are not merely talking about believing correct theology. We are talking about the whole being—spirit, soul, and body—coming into agreement under God's leadership.

Because Here is something literal and undeniable: if your spirit is reaching for God, but your soul is rehearsing panic, and your body is living on adrenaline and exhaustion, you will experience faith as strain instead of resonance. Not because God is absent, but because the inner world is divided.

Jesus models a whole—being life. He withdrew to pray (Mark 1:35). He slept in a storm (Mark 4:38). He fasted (Matthew 4:1–2). He wept (John 11:35). He set boundaries (Mark 1:37–38; John 2:24). He walked in compassion without being controlled by crowds. He lived integrated—spirit—led, mind anchored, body submitted.

Whole—being faith is not moral perfection. It is internal wholeness. It is when your spirit says, God is Lord, your mind says, His Word is true, your will says, I will obey, your emotions learn to follow truth instead of lead it, and your body becomes a servant instead of a dictator.

This is what Scripture calls integrity. Not that you never battle. Not that you never wrestle. But that you are not living divided.

James warns that the double—minded person is unstable (James 1:6–8). Double—mindedness is not only indecision; it is inner contradiction. One part reaches; another part resists. One part believes; another part rehearses fear. One part worships; another part clings to control.

Alignment is God bringing the whole being into agreement—so you stop vibrating in contradiction.

And here the ancient commandment becomes astonishingly modern: "Hear, O Israel: The Lord our God, the Lord is one. You shall love the Lord your God with all your heart, with all your soul, and with all your strength" (Deuteronomy 6:4–5). Jesus echoes it as the greatest commandment (Mark 12:29–30; Matthew 22:37). Notice what begins it: hear. Love is tethered to hearing. Not mere belief. Not mere knowledge. Hearing that becomes love.

Because love is not abstract. Love is agreement in motion.

When Jesus says this is the greatest commandment, He is not compressing faith into a slogan. He is restoring alignment to its purest form. The Lord is one. And the aligned life becomes one—not fragmented, not double—minded, not compartmentalized. Unity in God produces unity in us.

Broken Signals and Static — How misalignment occurs

Misalignment often begins with something that feels harmless. A slow drift. A crowded schedule. A heart that means well but never stops long enough to listen. Faith passed down without personal encounter can begin to sound like a radio station slipping off frequency—static growing, clarity fading, until what once felt alive becomes noise you tolerate.

But the broadcast has never failed. The problem has never been the signal. It has always been alignment.

This is where we must be painfully honest: many of us substitute genuine encounter with something less demanding than our whole being. We replace alignment with approximation—close enough to feel spiritual, not deep enough to transform. And the result is a weakened signal.

Sometimes the counterfeits are subtle. Sometimes they are culturally applauded. Sometimes they hide behind ministry language. Sometimes they hide behind intellect. But they all share one fruit: static.

There is a counterfeit power that operates without humility—revelation treated like possession, authority assumed instead of received. Pride as power. Power divorced from awe. Revelation claimed as entitlement. This is the root counterfeit because pride is always a refusal to be tuned; it insists on being the tuner.

There is familiarity mistaken for intimacy. Grace mistaken for permission. Closeness without reverence. Access is a gift. Entitlement is access without awe. It is approaching God as though He were obligated to our preferences.

There are emotional experiences mistaken for transformation. A moment of intensity mistaken for maturation. Feeling God mistaken for following God. Encounters that move emotions but never reshape obedience.

There is information mistaken for relationship—teaching replacing communion. This is especially dangerous for gifted thinkers and teachers, because insight can feel like intimacy when it is not. You can study God without submitting to God. You can explain holiness while avoiding surrender. You can talk about alignment while resisting it.

There are gifts operating without formation—calling mistaken for readiness, visibility mistaken for approval. Gifts are given freely; character is formed slowly (1 Corinthians 12:4–11; Galatians 5:22–23). And Jesus warns that activity in His name is not the same as knowing Him (Matthew 7:21–23).

There is spiritual control—attempting to harness spiritual principles, using prayer as leverage instead of communion, treating God like a system to manipulate. This is classic alchemy: If I do this, God must do that. **But God is not a mechanism. He is a Father.**

All of these produce the same outcome: static.

Static can be external. The busyness of life. Constant input. The endless noise that keeps the receiver from ever being still long enough to calibrate. Static can be internal. Unmanaged offense. Unhealed wounds. Fear. Shame. A mind trained to spiral. Static can be relational. Disconnection from others and from God. Scripture makes this painfully practical: "If someone says, 'I love God,' and hates his brother, he is a liar" (1 John 4:20–21). Love and alignment are linked. You cannot hate people made in God's image and pretend you are aligned with the God whose nature is love (1 John 4:8).

Static can be moral. Secret sin. Compromise. Quiet agreements with darkness. And static can be negligence. Spiritual laziness. Avoidance. The slow drift that happens when we stop returning to the Source.

Misalignment can also feel like collision inside the soul—two dominant voices competing, two messages pulsing. God speaks peace, but fear speaks panic. God speaks identity, but shame speaks accusation. God speaks truth, but offense speaks bitterness. When two voices compete, the soul becomes exhausted, not only because life is hard, but because the inner world is out of agreement.

The Garden of Eden reveals the beginning of this distortion. Eden was designed for fellowship. Yet an opposing voice lingered. Eve's first fracture was not first an action; it was listening. She attended to the wrong voice (Genesis 3:1–6). Deception entered. Disobedience followed. Shame rose. Fear hid (Genesis 3:7–10). The enemy rarely needs to silence God. He only needs to distort reception.

If hearing is the first command, distortion is the first tactic.

This is why Jesus' repeated phrase lands like a warning and an invitation: "He who has ears to hear, let him hear" (Mark 4:9; Matthew 11:15). It is not about biology. It is about alignment. It is about whether the heart is positioned to receive.

You can have ears and not hear. You can have Bibles and not discern. You can sit in sermons and still live in static. Because hearing is not exposure. It is reception.

So it becomes necessary to pause and ask, gently but honestly: Where have I substituted something less demanding than full alignment? Have I mistaken emotion for transformation? Information for intimacy? Gift for character? Familiarity for reverence? Control for surrender? If my signal has been weak, what static have I normalized?

God does not ask these questions to shame you. He asks them to heal you.

Repentance as Realignment — Turning back into resonance

What if repentance is not what you were trained to fear, but what you were created to return through?

Sometimes repentance begins as nothing more dramatic than a gentle shift of posture. A soft turning of attention. A quiet decision to come back toward the Lord—not to earn Him, but to face Him again. In essence, that is repentance. And as He meets us there, He begins to soften our assumptions about His motives, His character, and His intentions. Distortion lifts, not because we suddenly perfected ourselves, but because we became willing to know Him as He is meant to be known, to hear Him as He is meant to be heard.

If your history with repentance has been heavy—if it has felt like groveling, shame, or spiritual scolding—let this be a new doorway. Repentance is not humiliation. Repentance is healing. Repentance is mercy because it is the moment you stop agreeing with distortion and start agreeing with Truth again.

Religion sometimes turns repentance into a courtroom scene. Guilty. Condemned. Disappointed God. Do better. Feel worse. But the gospel reveals something else. God is not inviting you into a spiral. He is inviting you into cleansing. "If we confess our sins, He is faithful and just to forgive us our sins and to cleanse us from all unrighteousness" (1 John 1:9). Forgiveness is paired with cleansing. Not only pardon, but restoration.

Sin can be understood, in its simplest form, as whatever separates us from God. It is rebellion, yes, but its immediate fruit is distance, distortion, interference. James writes that stumbling at one point makes one guilty of all (James 2:10). Not because all sins carry the same earthly consequence, but because they share the same spiritual problem: they disrupt fellowship with holiness.

And yet even this is not written to crush you. It is written to bring you home. Because if sin separates, repentance reconnects.

The Psalmist describes God's forgiveness with extravagant distance: "As far as the east is from the west, so far has He removed our transgressions from us" (Psalm 103:12). God's forgiveness is not reluctant. It is removal. He does not merely cover sin and store it somewhere for later accusation. He casts it away from your identity and your relationship with Him.

Repentance, then, is return. It is realignment. It is turning back into resonance.

Sometimes the language of waves can help us feel what Scripture is saying without trying to "prove" God through physics. When a life is out of alignment, it experiences dissonance. The inner world cancels itself. Peace feels distant. Clarity feels lost. The person says, I believe, and yet something inside is fighting.

But the distance is not proof of God's absence. It is proof of interference.

Repentance is the mercy of God because it is the return to agreement. It is the moment your inner life stops opposing God's voice and begins to rise and fall with it again. It is the removal of static. It is the restoration of clarity. Not because God finally decided to come close, but because you stopped running competing frequencies inside your own heart.

And this is where it becomes deeply personal, and sometimes deeply physical. Why do we sometimes feel God's presence? Why are some more aware of it than others?

This is not a contest of spirituality. It is often a matter of attunement.

Our bodies register what our souls are hosting. Anxiety tightens muscles. Peace softens the breath. Shame collapses the posture. Joy lifts the face. The body is a witness. It is not your enemy; it is your dashboard. It often reveals what the spirit is fighting.

If your body cannot rest, you may be agreeing with control.
If your body is always tense, you may be agreeing with fear.
If your appetites are ungoverned, you may be agreeing with comfort as

lord. If your schedule has no space for God, you may be agreeing with self—sufficiency.

Not shame. Just truth.

God is kind enough to show us where alignment is needed. Often the body becomes the dashboard light, not to condemn, but to invite. The goal is not to silence symptoms. The goal is to return to the Source.

"Be still and know that I am God" (Psalm 46:10). **Stillness is not emptiness. Stillness is tuning.** God is not impressed by quiet people; He is calling busy Hearts to come home. Stillness reduces noise. Stillness restores sensitivity. Stillness makes space for the heart to remember what it already knows deep down: God is present, God is speaking, and God is near.

When repentance becomes return, you realize something breathtaking. God is not withholding Himself from you. He is inviting you back into agreement with what has been true all along.

Remaining Tuned — Sustaining clarity in a noisy world

So how do we stay aligned? How do we remain tuned when life is loud and the soul is easily crowded?

Perhaps the answer is simpler than we fear. Not easy, but simple.

The tuned life is not a life without noise. It is a life that knows how to return quickly.

Scripture gives us a picture of this return in a quiet house where two sisters respond to Jesus in two very different ways. Martha is busy—serving, preparing, managing, carrying the weight of what must be done. Mary sits at His feet, listening. And Jesus says Mary has chosen the better portion, "the one thing needed," the portion that will not be taken away (Luke 10:38–42).

Before action comes presence. Before assignment comes alignment. Before doing comes hearing.

This is not a rebuke of service. It is a revelation of sequence. You can do much for Jesus and still drift from Jesus. You can labor in His name and still be spiritually misaligned. It is possible to confuse activity with communion.

Remaining tuned begins with returning to the feet of Jesus.

"Draw near to God, and He will draw near to you" (James 4:8). This is not a performance contract; it is a relational reality. Proximity changes perception. The more you remain near the Source, the more your inner rhythms begin to align. A life lived far from His presence will drift—not because God moved, but because you did.

Remaining tuned also involves protecting the channel. "Guard your heart" (Proverbs 4:23) is not only moral advice; it is spiritual wisdom. What you allow into your eyes, mind, emotions, and imagination becomes part of your inner environment. You cannot live on constant noise and expect sensitivity to remain intact. You cannot saturate your soul with chaos and expect clarity to be effortless. You cannot normalize static and still claim you want a clean signal.

Purity is not just moral cleanliness; it is clarity of channel. It includes repentance when sin interrupts resonance (1 John 1:9). It includes forgiveness when bitterness hardens the heart (Ephesians 4:31–32). It includes guarding what you entertain in your mind. It includes choosing stillness when distraction is devouring your awareness.

And purpose follows naturally from hearing. Jesus says, "My sheep hear My voice… and they follow Me" (John 10:27). Following is not forced labor; it is the movement of resonance. When you hear clearly, obedience becomes less about pressure and more about response.

Remaining tuned also requires humility—the pliability that keeps you tunable. "God resists the proud but gives grace to the humble" (James 4:6; 1 Peter 5:5–6). Pride is the refusal to be corrected. Pride is the demand to stay in control. Pride is the insistence that your interpretation must be right. Humility is the willingness to be tuned—even when it costs you your preferred narrative.

And woven through all of this is the simplest sustaining force of all: love.

Jesus summarizes the whole law with love—love God with all your heart, soul, mind, and strength; love your neighbor as yourself (Matthew 22:37–39). Then He makes it even more personal: "Love one another as I have loved you" (John 13:34–35). Faith works through love (Galatians 5:6). Love is not a side virtue. Love is the central reality of the Kingdom. Love is alignment made visible.

And Scripture refuses to leave love undefined. "Love is patient, love is kind… it rejoices with the truth… it bears all things, believes all things, hopes all things, endures all things" (1 Corinthians 13:4–7). This is not sentimental poetry. It is a diagnostic. It shows what is governing the inner life. Because love—biblical love—is the whole—being response that keeps the heart tuned.

Love makes space for God. Love makes space for people. Love refuses the static of bitterness, the distortion of pride, the interference of self—protection that masquerades as wisdom. Love keeps returning. Love keeps softening. Love keeps listening.

And worship becomes the posture that restores love's center.

Worship is not performance; it is surrender. It is the whole being remembering we are not the origin. He is. We are echoes, created to receive His voice and release it back into the world with Heaven's weight behind it. Worship is not merely singing; it is resonance. It is the soul kneeling. It is the mind yielding. It is the body offering itself as a living sacrifice (Romans 12:1).

In Isaiah's vision, you can see the rhythm that keeps a life tuned: upward—behold Him; inward—be cleansed; outward—be sent (Isaiah 6:1–8). Revelation, repentance, response. Again and again. This cycle keeps the heart aligned because it keeps the heart surrendered.

And resonance does not end inside you. It ripples.

A single drop touches still water and circles expand outward. The surface becomes a living language: the entire body of water responding to one point of contact. Faith moves like that. When divine presence touches the human spirit, what begins as a quiet vibration becomes a wave of transformation. And then your life—your words, your choices, your prayers, your love—begins to touch others in ways you cannot always measure but can often see.

In a noisy world, remaining tuned is not accidental. It is chosen. It is protected. It is practiced. And it is returned to.

If you have felt distant, confused, heavy, or spiritually "off," do not interpret that as God abandoning you. Interpret it as feedback. A signal can be restored. A receiver can be retuned. A heart can be brought back into agreement.

The broadcast has never stopped. God is still speaking.

And alignment—true alignment—is your return to what you were designed for: spirit to Spirit, whole being, fully loved, fully listening, fully alive. If you have made it here, something may already be stirring. The same Voice that spoke creation into being is calling your name—not into the air, but into the inner chambers of your heart.

You were not meant to only read about the Sound of God. You were meant to resonate with it. The invitation is not to ritual. It is to relationship. It is to say, in the simplest and truest way, Yes, Lord—I hear You. I believe. I receive You.

"If you confess with your mouth that Jesus is Lord and believe in your heart that God raised Him from the dead, you will be saved" (Romans 10:9). And as you answer, something unseen shifts. Not because you earned a new standing, but because you returned to the One who has been standing there all along.

Sit in this truth for a moment—Selah. Pause. Listen closely. That quiet beneath the noise, that peace that wasn't there before, that sense of homecoming—this is the resonance of reconciliation. You have not just read the Word; you have received Him. And from this day forward, let your life resound with the glory of the One who spoke light into existence.

You have heard. Now stay aligned.

Return often. Now you will understand your Assignment.

Enter your Assignment.

ASSIGNMENT

You Were Tuned on Purpose

Picture a serene body of water before the pebble falls.

Not the dramatic kind of ocean, already busy with whitecaps and wind, but a quiet pond in the early morning, glassy enough to reflect the sky like a held breath. In that kind of stillness, even a small touch becomes a message. The surface receives the impact and translates it into circles—clean, widening rings that carry the signature of that first contact.

It makes me wonder if this is why God so often leads us into stillness before He leads us into anything else. Not because He is withholding, but because stillness is the condition in which His movement can be perceived. Turbulent water will swallow the energy of a stone; turbulent souls will swallow the gentleness of a whisper. It isn't that God can't speak over the noise. It's that we often can't tell which wave is His.

The ripple also exposes another truth: impact is not mainly about size. It is about contact, and timing, and the integrity of the surface that receives it. A stone thrown with intent carries momentum; a pebble released without attention barely disturbs the skin of the water. In the same way, a word spoken from depth carries farther than a thousand words spoken from hurry. The difference is not volume. It is alignment.

The strange part is that alignment often feels simple once you taste it, and nearly impossible while you are searching for it. You can spend years trying to manufacture peace, only to discover that peace arrives when you stop trying to manufacture anything at all. You return to the center of His will—sometimes through repentance, sometimes through a quiet surrender, sometimes through one honest prayer—and suddenly you realize you have been living at the edges of yourself. You were designed for a different center. You were tuned for a different steadiness. There is a place where His voice positions you, and your soul can finally exhale.

When that happens, purpose stops feeling like a hunt. It starts feeling like home. Not because life gets easy, but because your inner world gets coherent. You stop thrashing for meaning and begin to receive meaning as a gift. And once you find it, you become protective of it—not in fear, but in reverence, because you recognize how quickly spiritual noise can blur the signal.

My father—in—law once told me, "To God, time means nothing; but timing is everything." I have found it to be strangely true. God is rarely early by our measurements, rarely late by our anxieties, and yet uncannily precise. Perhaps timing is His quality control for impact. A word released too soon can bruise. A word released too late can miss. But a word released in His moment can travel farther than we can track.

And then, quietly, the thought turns personal: what if design precedes destiny? What if you were tuned on purpose?

Genesis opens with a scene that feels like that still pond: deep waters, darkness, and the Spirit of God hovering—present, attentive, poised over potential (Genesis 1:2). Then the first divine act is speech. "And God said…" (Genesis 1:3). Before light was seen, sound was released. Before form appeared, the Word moved across the surface.

Could it be that God made us in His image not only in moral capacity, relational hunger, or creative intelligence, but also in this strange, sacred ability to carry voice? Scripture does not romanticize our words; it warns us about them. That warning itself is a kind of compliment. You do not warn someone about something insignificant. You warn them because it has weight.

As a vocal instructor, I've spent years helping people "find their voice." Not just their volume, or their performance persona, but the sound that belongs to them. It's humbling, because every person carries a unique instrument. A voice is not a generic tool. It is a signature.

From a physical standpoint, the voice is born in vibration. Breath rises from the lungs, passes through the larynx, and sets the vocal folds into rapid oscillation; sound waves emerge, then get shaped by tongue, lips, teeth, and the resonant cavities of the throat and face. Voice is breath meeting vibration, then becoming intelligible sound.

It's startling how close that is to Genesis: Spirit hovering, then speech, then creation. The voice is not "made" by the vocal folds alone; it is released when breath and vibration meet.

If that is true, then your voice is more than a communication device. It is a witness to divine design. You were made to take what is unseen—thought, intention, love, faith—and translate it into the air so another person can receive it.

And here is where reverence begins to replace casualness. **If we are, in any measure, an extension of God's voice in the earth, then speech is not neutral. The words that leave our mouths do not simply pass the time; they shape the atmosphere we live inside.**

Calling Is Frequency—Specific

There is a phenomenon in physics often demonstrated with tuning forks. Strike one fork tuned to a certain pitch, and another fork of the same natural frequency can begin vibrating as well—without being struck. It "recognizes" the frequency. It responds. This is sympathetic resonance.

When I first watched that demonstration, it felt like a parable. A note released in the room awakens a note already "tuned" to it. The second fork doesn't strain to respond; it simply does. It does not compete with the first; it resonates with it.

Could calling work like that? Could God's assignments be frequency—specific?

If so, comparison is not merely an emotional trap; it is a spiritual detuning. When you fixate on someone else's sound, you begin to adjust your own pitch to match theirs, and the cost is quiet at first. You feel effort where there used to be ease. You feel restlessness that can't be explained.

Comparison breaks alignment because it invites you to carry a frequency you were not designed to carry. A choir doesn't become powerful because every singer insists on the same melody line. It becomes powerful when each voice holds its part and listens for the whole.

The Scriptures that warn us about the tongue are not threats to paralyze us; they are invitations to honor design.

"Death and life are in the power of the tongue" (Proverbs 18:21). That sentence suggests speech is not merely descriptive; it is generative. We don't create ex nihilo the way God does, but we do participate in creating environments—internal and external—through what we release.

"And God said, 'Let there be light,' and there was light" (Genesis 1:3). The pattern is clear: God speaks, and reality responds. When we speak in alignment with His heart, something responds as well—sometimes in someone else, sometimes in our own courage, sometimes in the atmosphere of a home.

Jesus took words with even greater seriousness. "Everyone will have to give account… for every empty word they have spoken. For by your words you will be acquitted, and by your words you will be condemned" (Matthew 12:36–37). He wasn't saying God is petty. He was saying words reveal and steer the soul. Speech is not separate from identity; it's one of the clearest mirrors of it.

If calling is frequency—specific, then our daily question is not "How loud can I be?" but "How aligned am I?" Not "How impressive is my sound?" but "Is my sound true?"

Stewarding the Signal

If design precedes destiny, then stewardship precedes impact.

Scripture treats the mind, heart, and mouth as an interconnected system. Paul writes, "Be transformed by the renewing of your mind" (Romans 12:2). Jesus says, "Out of the abundance of the heart the mouth speaks" (Luke 6:45). Wisdom urges, "Above all else, guard your heart, for everything you do flows from it" (Proverbs 4:23). What we allow into the mind becomes a filter; what settles in the heart becomes conviction; what exits the mouth becomes atmosphere.

I used to think transformation happened simply by exposure to information. If I heard enough sermons, read enough books, gathered enough verses, surely, I would be changed. But information is not automatically formation. You can hear the same truth for years and still live as if it isn't true. Then the issue isn't content alone. It's the condition of the inner receiver.

That's why Scripture doesn't only say, "Renew your mind." It also says, "Be filled with the Spirit… speaking to one another in psalms, hymns, and spiritual songs, singing and making melody in your **Heart** to the Lord" (Ephesians 5:18–19). Notice the movement. Filling leads to speaking. Singing leads to inner melody. Sound is not just outward; it becomes inward.

James warns that "the tongue is a small member… it is a fire" (James 3:5–6). Small things can steer large systems. A sentence can redirect a marriage. A muttered self—curse can redirect a lifetime.

In wave physics, interference describes what happens when waves meet. When two waves are in phase, their amplitudes add and the result is stronger; this is constructive interference. When they are out of phase, they partially or fully cancel; this is destructive interference.

Spiritual life has its own kind of interference. When our inner life and our outer speech are in phase—when what we believe, love, and say move together—the result is coherence. But when we live out of phase, we leak. We declare trust while nursing fear. We sing surrender while gripping control. That dissonance doesn't only sound unpleasant; it weakens our capacity to carry revelation.

Stewarding the signal means taking responsibility for what we transmit. It means refusing to curse ourselves with "honesty," and refusing to bless our anxiety with spiritual language. It means learning to speak truth without using truth as a weapon.

One of the most tender battlegrounds is the way we talk about ourselves. We can preach grace to others and still speak condemnation over our own Hearts. We can quote promises in public and privately narrate our lives with despair. Yet Jesus tied speech to the deep reservoir of the heart: "Out of the abundance of the heart the mouth speaks" (Luke 6:45). If that is true, then a harsh tongue is not only a social issue; it is a diagnostic. It reveals what has been stored. It reveals what we are trusting. It reveals what we believe God thinks about us.

This is why renewal is never only about new information. Renewal is about a new inner atmosphere. It is about letting truth soak past the mind and settle into the heart until it becomes instinct. It is about re—training the soul to recognize God's tone as familiar, and the enemy's accusations as foreign. And sometimes that training looks very ordinary: returning to Scripture when the mind spirals, worshiping when the emotions resist, choosing silence before releasing a reactive sentence, blessing someone when your flesh wants to bruise them with sarcasm.

We learn the responsibility of revelation here. If God has entrusted you with His word, His presence, His Spirit, then you do not get to treat speech casually. You begin to ask, quietly, before you speak: is this aligned? Is this true? Is this loving? Is this necessary? Not as a legalistic fear, but as a reverent awareness that your words carry weight in the unseen.

Movement That Flows From Listening

There is a kind of obedience that feels like pressure, and there is a kind of obedience that feels like overflow. The difference is listening.

"Deep calls to deep" (Psalm 42:7). That line has always felt like more than poetry. It feels like a description of resonance—something in God calling to something in us, something eternal recognizing what is eternal.

In the study of coupled oscillators, synchronization can occur simply because systems share a connection. One of the most famous early observations came from Christiaan Huygens, who noted in 1665 that two pendulum clocks mounted on the same structure could fall into synchronized motion.

Modern demonstrations make it tangible. Place multiple metronomes on a movable base, start them at different tempos, and over time they often synchronize. The shared base couples their motion; the system finds a common rhythm.

This is entrainment—separate rhythms gently pulling toward shared timing through proximity and connection.

I can't help but see the spiritual parallel. God does not usually change us by shouting at us from a distance. He draws near. He invites us closer. "Draw near to God, and He will draw near to you" (James 4:8). The longer we remain near, the more our scattered inner tempos begin to adjust. Our frantic metronomes start to slow. Our grief begins to breathe.

Not because we were coerced into peace, but because we were close enough to be influenced by it.

This is why Psalm 46:10 lands like a key in a lock: "Be still and know that I am God." Stillness isn't laziness. Stillness is attunement. It is giving the soul a stable surface so it can feel the subtle pull of God's rhythm.

Jesus illustrated this with Mary and Martha. Martha was busy serving; Mary was seated, listening. Martha complained, and Jesus answered with gentle clarity: "You are anxious and troubled about many things, but one thing is necessary. Mary has chosen the good portion" (Luke 10:41–42). He didn't shame service. He re—ordered priority. The "one thing" was proximity.

And here is where obedience becomes overflow. When you've been near enough to feel His heart, you don't obey to earn love; you obey because love has tuned you. You move because the rhythm has entered you.

Becoming a Living Echo

If you were tuned on purpose, and if calling is frequency—specific, and if stewardship protects clarity, then the question becomes beautifully simple: what does it mean to carry God's sound into the world?

It means you become a living echo.

An echo is not original sound; it is original sound carried into new space. That is what witness is. It is not inventing God. It is reflecting Him.

Scripture describes moments when unified worship carried a weight that felt like a threshold opening. When "the trumpeters and singers were as one… then the house of the Lord was filled" with glory (2 Chronicles 5:13–14). The pattern is unmistakable: alignment precedes manifestation.

In that light, division becomes more than disagreement. It becomes dissonance—destructive interference in the unseen.

So becoming a living echo involves humility. It involves listening for the pitch of Heaven and refusing to sing in a key that flatters ego but fractures harmony. It involves honoring other callings without trying to absorb them. It involves letting love, not visibility, define success.

And then—because the gospel is never only metaphor—it involves a personal response.

Jesus does not invite you to admire Him from afar. He invites you to follow. "My sheep hear my voice, and I know them, and they follow me" (John 10:27). And like a refrain through Revelation, "He who has an ear, let him hear what the Spirit says" (Revelation 2:7).

"If you confess with your mouth that Jesus is Lord and believe in your heart that God raised Him from the dead, you will be saved" (Romans 10:9). Confession is not a magic formula; it is alignment.

Jesus, I hear You. I believe You are the Son of God. I believe You came for me, died for me, and rose again. I open every chamber of my heart to You. Forgive me, renew me, and teach me to recognize Your voice. Tune my life to Your truth. Let my life carry Your sound into the world.

And if you prayed that, then pause. Let the stillness be the witness that something has shifted.

Because the gospel does not stop at forgiveness; it continues into presence.

After His resurrection, Jesus breathed on His disciples and said, "Receive the Holy Spirit" (John 20:22). Breath again. Spirit again. The Creator exhaling restoration. Paul tells believers they are "sealed with the promised Holy Spirit" (Ephesians 1:13), and that their bodies are temples—dwelling places—of that Spirit (1 Corinthians 6:19). God does not only speak to you. He chooses to live in you.

Life in the Spirit is not mainly a dramatic moment; it is a steady companionship. Jesus promised the Spirit would guide us into truth (John 16:13). Paul said the Spirit bears witness with our spirit that we are children of God (Romans 8:16). Sometimes that witness arrives as a sudden clarity. Sometimes it arrives as a restrained word you didn't say. Sometimes it arrives as peace that guards your mind when circumstances still shake. You begin to recognize that guidance is often quiet, and that the Spirit's steadiness is rarely frantic. He does not yank you into holiness; He draws you into it, patiently, consistently, like a rhythm you slowly learn to trust.

That is why the New Testament speaks not only of being indwelt but of being filled. "Be filled with the Spirit" (Ephesians 5:18). Filled implies capacity. It implies room. It implies surrender.

Some believers experience this filling in ways that include a new kind of prayer language, as in Acts 2 when the disciples "were all filled with the Holy Spirit and began to speak in other tongues as the Spirit gave them utterance" (Acts 2:4). Paul describes praying in tongues as "uttering mysteries in the Spirit" (1 Corinthians 14:2), and he speaks of the Spirit helping us in weakness when words fail (Romans 8:26). However you understand these gifts, the invitation remains: God gives nearness, and nearness changes us.

Perhaps that is the deepest meaning of assignment. Not a to—do list from God, but a life lived in phase with Him. A heart close enough to entrain to His steadiness. A mind renewed enough to filter truth. A mouth disciplined enough to release life.

And then, naturally, movement flows.

You begin to notice moments when your words carry unusual gentleness. You notice that you no longer need to win as much as you need to be true. Prayer becomes less like shouting into the heavens and more like breathing with God. Your "yes" feels lighter, because it is not pushed by fear; it is pulled by love.

This is quiet transformation. This is the ripple effect. A life tuned to Heaven does not only change itself; it changes its surroundings. Like that second tuning fork across the room, another heart begins to vibrate, not because you forced it, but because you carried a frequency they could recognize.

So here is the closing wonder: what if your assignment is not primarily about doing more, but about becoming clearer? What if the world is not starving for louder Christians, but for truer ones? What if God's voice—steady as eternity—is already hovering over the deep places in you, waiting for your stillness, waiting for your consent, waiting for your simple, reverent "yes"?

May your mind be renewed (Romans 12:2). May your heart be guarded and softened (Proverbs 4:23). May your mouth be an altar where life is released (Proverbs 18:21). May your obedience be the overflow of listening (Luke 10:41–42). And may the sound you carry be so aligned with Jesus that others, without knowing why, feel their own hearts begin to awaken in response.

Proof Beyond Persuasion

There is a kind of spiritual tragedy that keeps replaying itself in the modern world: people hear Christians speak the language of love, but what they most often feel from Christians is judgment. Not the steady, clarifying kind of moral light that exposes what harms us so we can be healed, but the sharp, reactive kind of condemnation that feels like rejection wearing religious clothes. And if we're honest, many are no longer rejecting Jesus first. They are rejecting the emotional atmosphere they've learned to associate with His people.

It makes me wonder if this is why so many conversations about faith go nowhere. We keep trying to persuade minds while our lives quietly contradict the message. We try to convince the intellect while our tone betrays our center. We attempt to win arguments about Love while radiating fear, suspicion, impatience, and offense. And the world—already exhausted by noise—has become astonishingly sensitive to dissonance. It can forgive ignorance faster than hypocrisy. It can tolerate questions better than posturing. But it struggles to trust a gospel that sounds like grace and feels like contempt.

Jesus gave the world a different measuring stick. He didn't say, "They will know you are Mine by your precision." He didn't say, "They will know you are Mine by how thoroughly you can debate." He said, "By this all people will know that you are My disciples, if you have love for one another" (John 13:35). And love, in Scripture, is not mere sentiment. Love has texture. Love has restraint. Love has patience. Love carries a holy steadiness. Love is recognizable.

Perhaps the most convincing proof to the world is not our ability to describe God, but the evidence of a life rooted in Him. Not the performance of spirituality, but the presence of peace. Not the spectacle of certainty, but the quiet center that remains even when everything shakes.

This is where the gospel becomes embodied rather than advertised. This is where faith becomes visible without becoming loud. This is where our assignment stops being a strenuous attempt to prove ourselves and becomes the overflow of a life aligned with God.

When Paul prays that believers would be "rooted and grounded in love" (Ephesians 3:17), it reads like more than encouragement. It reads like architecture. Roots are what hold a tree steady when wind attacks.

Grounding is what keeps a system stable when power surges. A rooted life is not easily toppled by criticism, by chaos, by the emotional weather of an anxious age. And grounded love is not fragile. It does not evaporate when people disappoint you. It does not mutate into rage when your worldview is threatened. Rooted, grounded love holds.

So what does it look like to live our faith out loud in a way that doesn't coerce, bribe, or intimidate, but actually reveals the Father?

It may be simpler—and more costly—than we thought.

Living faith out loud requires Alignment, Arbitration, and Abiding.

Alignment is the posture of being tuned. It is the daily returning of the inner life to the voice of God—letting His Word and Spirit set our pitch. "My sheep hear My voice" (John 10:27) isn't only about guidance; it's about familiarity. Which voice do I recognize most quickly? Which tone do I obey most naturally? And what does my nervous system do when I am not aligned—when I'm spiritually off—key and don't want to admit it?

Arbitration is what happens when multiple voices compete for authority inside you. It is the sober, Spirit—led discernment that chooses which voice gets to interpret reality. The world is loud with narratives, outrage cycles, fear scripts, and endless accusations. Your own memories can accuse you. Your own shame can preach to you. Even religious environments can put pressure on you to perform instead of abide.

Arbitration is the act of letting Christ be the Judge of your inner court. It is taking every competing thought and asking, "Is this true? Is this from God? Does this align with Scripture? Does this produce the fruit of the Spirit, or the fruit of the flesh?" (Galatians 5:22–23). It is refusing to let a reactive impulse masquerade as righteous zeal.

And **Abiding** is the deepest layer—the being that must always precede doing. "Abide in Me, and I in you… apart from Me you can do nothing" (John 15:4–5). Nothing does not mean you can't produce activity. It means you can't produce eternal fruit. You can build platforms, gather crowds, and win arguments while your soul is slowly hollowing out. But abiding produces a different kind of life: a life that bears fruit because it is connected.

This is why the doing must always flow from the being. When we reverse the order, we become spiritual laborers with no oil. We become Christians who know the right words but carry the wrong spirit. We become voices without presence, sound without resonance.

It's sobering to realize how easy it is to substitute knowledge for witness. Knowledge matters, yes. Peter tells us to be ready to give an answer for the hope within us (1 Peter 3:15). But He doesn't stop there—He adds the manner: "with gentleness and respect" (1 Peter 3:15). There is a way to speak truth that feels like love, and a way to speak "truth" that feels like domination. The difference is not vocabulary; it is spirit.

Paul warns that "knowledge puffs up, but love builds up" (1 Corinthians 8:1). That single line exposes a common pitfall of modern Christianity: we can be correct and still be un—Christlike. We can be doctrinally sharp and relationally unsafe. We can be biblically literate and emotionally unhealed. We can speak about the Prince of Peace while living as ambassadors of anxiety.

And the world notices.

It notices when our faith produces outrage more naturally than compassion. It notices when we discuss grace but default to suspicion. It notices when we speak about forgiveness but refuse to listen. It notices when we talk about holiness but use shame as a weapon. It notices when our "discernment" is simply cynicism in church clothes.

Jesus warned about this posture with frightening clarity: "First take the log out of your own eye" (Matthew 7:5). Not because self—examination is a cute spiritual exercise, but because an unexamined soul cannot see clearly enough to help anyone else. When we avoid our own transformation, we eventually turn ministry into projection. We punish people for the places we refuse to heal.

So perhaps the modern world does not need Christians who are louder. Perhaps it needs Christians who are truer. Christians whose lives make the Father believable again.

What would it look like if the evidence we offered was peace?

Not denial. Not escapism. Not a plastic smile. But the kind of peace that surpasses understanding (Philippians 4:7). The kind of peace that can grieve without collapsing. The kind of peace that can confront without contempt. The kind of peace that remains centered even when the world—or your world—seems to be falling apart.

Scripture dares to describe this stability as a promised reality: "You keep him in perfect peace whose mind is stayed on You, because He trusts in You" (Isaiah 26:3). Stayed. Anchored. Held. That is not the peace of perfect circumstances; it is the peace of a mind that has learned where to rest. And if that peace becomes visible in you, it becomes proof beyond persuasion. It becomes the gospel made tangible.

In a culture addicted to outrage, a steady Christian is strange. In a culture trained to escalate, a gentle Christian is disruptive. In a culture that assumes everyone has an angle, a transparent Christian is disarming. And that is exactly the point. The Kingdom advances with a different kind of power.

This is where good works find their rightful place. Jesus says, "Let your light shine before others, so that they may see your good works and give glory to your Father who is in Heaven" (Matthew 5:16). Notice where the spotlight lands. Not on you. Not on your virtue. Not on your moral superiority. On the Father. Good works are not meant to coerce people into compliance or scare them into agreement. They are meant to reveal what the Father is like.

If that's true, then we have to admit another modern pitfall: we can use "good works" as a form of control. We can serve with strings attached. We can love people as a strategy rather than a posture. We can give in order to be seen. We can "help" as a way to feel superior. But love that is rooted in God is free of manipulation because it is not trying to extract something from the other person. It is simply bearing witness to the Giver.

So the question becomes intensely practical: how do we remain in continued alignment with God so our lives naturally affect the world around us?

Maybe we begin by asking better questions in the quiet.

When I feel the urge to correct someone, am I moved by love or by irritation? "The anger of man does not produce the righteousness of God" (James 1:20). If my tone is heated, why? What am I protecting? What fear is hiding under my need to be right?

When I talk about sin, do people feel invited into repentance or pushed into shame? Paul tells us, "God's kindness is meant to lead you to repentance" (Romans 2:4). If kindness leads, then cruelty cannot be justified as zeal.

When I speak online or in public, do my words sound like the Spirit of Christ, "gentle and lowly in heart" (Matthew 11:29), or do they sound like the spirit of accusation? Scripture calls Satan "the accuser" (Revelation 12:10). That alone should make us tremble before we baptize accusation as discernment.

When life feels unstable, do I return to abiding, or do I compensate with activity? Jesus says, "Abide in My love" (John 15:9). Not abide in your momentum. Not abide in your productivity. Abide in love. If love is the place, then frantic striving is a sign that I've wandered from the place.

When anxiety rises, do I treat it as normal, or as a signal that my inner court needs arbitration? Paul gives a concrete path: "Do not be anxious… but in everything by prayer and supplication with thanksgiving let your requests be made known to God. And the peace of God… will guard your Hearts and your minds" (Philippians 4:6–7). Peace is not merely a feeling; it is a guard. It stands at the door of the heart and mind. It keeps the signal clear.

When I'm tempted to prove myself, do I remember that the truest proof is fruit? "The fruit of the Spirit is love, joy, peace…" (Galatians 5:22). Fruit grows. It cannot be faked for long. It is slow evidence. It is living proof.

This is the threshold the modern world is waiting to see. Not Christians who have never suffered, but Christians whose suffering did not make them cruel. Not Christians who never feel anger, but Christians who refuse to be ruled by it. Not Christians who never face chaos, but Christians whose inner life is anchored somewhere deeper than circumstances.

That kind of life does not persuade; it attracts. It does not argue; it witnesses. It does not dominate; it shines.

And perhaps that is what assignment was always meant to be: not striving to do impressive things for God but learning to stay so aligned with God that what you do becomes the natural overflow of who you are becoming.

Alignment. Arbitration. Abiding.

If we will live there—truly live there—then even when our world shakes, something in us remains steady. And that steadiness becomes a sound the world has not heard in a long time: the sound of a soul at rest in God.

That sound is proof beyond persuasion.

Connection through encounter.
Consecration through alignment.
Commission through assignment.

These movements woven throughout this book point to one central truth: **God's voice brings us to life and gives us purpose.**

My hope is that as you conclude this journey of learning the *Sound of God*, you feel more compelled than ever by the intentionality of your design. You were not formed randomly or without care. You were created with purpose. You are deeply loved and designed with magnificent complexity.

And it is only fitting, then, to lean back toward the Creator in order to discover the fullness of who you were meant to be.

Your purpose does not begin someday in the distant future. It unlocks here and now.

You have learned how to listen. You have learned how to recognize the signal. And now you will begin to hear the Sound of God echoed throughout creation—in Scripture, in stillness, in the quiet witness of truth, and in the lives of those who walk in alignment with Him.

Each time you recognize that sound, reverence awakens again. And in that reverence, something inside you is drawn back to the One who first spoke life into being.

What an extraordinary Creator—to sustain the universe by His Word, and yet to hold every human life by His breath. When the breath that sustains you begins to recognize the Voice that formed you, agreement becomes the most natural response. Agreement with His voice sets alignment in motion – not just in you but in everything around you.

As the final movement of this journey, we join that Voice—

Declaring the Axioms of our faith.

Enter the Axioms.

AXIOM

Laws of Faith and Decree — *Unchanging spiritual principles that govern resonance*

There comes a moment when instruction must give way to agreement.

Not because teaching has failed, but because revelation has done what it was sent to do: it has brought you to a threshold where truth is no longer merely something you understand—it is something you can *inhabit.* Up to this point, you have been invited to listen, to discern, to quiet the noise, to recognize the difference between a counterfeit signal and the true Sound of God. You've been led, gently but steadily, toward the realization that God is not distant or abstract, not moody or withholding—He is present, intentional, communicative, and faithful to be known.

And now, in this chapter, the tone turns. Not away from wonder—but into a holy kind of certainty. Not certainty that pretends to have solved God, but certainty that has finally stopped fighting the invitation to trust Him.

Because transformation does not occur when truth is merely observed. Transformation occurs when truth is finally *agreed with.*

This is why axioms matter. They are not inspirational phrases; they are spiritual realities you can return to when your mind tries to drift back into confusion. They answer the questions that arise when a shift has occurred and you don't yet have language for it: *What happened to me? Why do I think differently now? What changed? What are the goal posts now? What am I living by?*

An axiom does not argue its validity—it simply is.

Gravity does not require belief to operate. Resonance does not require awareness to occur.
And the Kingdom of God is not built on chaos, but on unchanging truth.

So consider this chapter a sealing. A gathering in. A reverent "yes" spoken back to everything God has been whispering, illuminating, and aligning within you as you have read. If you feel refreshed, less confused, more rooted in the Word, more steady in your spirit, and somehow, mysteriously carried into a place of clarity you didn't manufacture… you have encountered the Sound of God.

And if you have made it all the way Here, let that completion mean something: not pride, but readiness. Not perfection, but posture. Not arrival, but *availability*. Completing this journey signals your willingness to hear more of His voice.

You are not just a listener.
You are the echo.

Why God Works Through Law — Love Expressed Through Order

Perhaps you once imagined that "law" meant distance. That it belonged to a colder version of God—rigid, untouchable, easily offended. But what if law, in the hands of a faithful Father, is not harshness… but *mercy with structure*?

God works through law not because He is rigid, but because He is reliable. Law is love made dependable. Order is compassion made trustworthy. Without law, love becomes unpredictable. Without structure, relationship becomes unstable. And without steadiness, intimacy becomes frightening—because you never know what you're going to get.

But God is not unstable.

His consistency is what makes nearness possible. You can draw close because He will not change into someone else when you do. You can confess honestly because He is not waiting to weaponize your weakness. You can learn His voice because it does not contradict His nature.

This is one of the most tender truths hidden inside the idea of spiritual law: God's "unchanging" is not a threat. It is an embrace you can rest inside.

And if this book has done anything at all, perhaps it has made this clear: God does not change frequencies.

What changes is us.

We tune. We drift. We distort. We return. We learn how to become still enough to notice what was always true. We realize that the problem was not His silence—it was our saturation. Not His absence—but our misalignment. Not His unwillingness to speak—but our habit of listening for Him in places He never promised to be.

An axiom is not a lecture. It's a lighthouse. Something that stands when emotions surge and storms rise. Something you can look at and say, "That is still true."

Faith as Agreement With Heaven — Alignment Produces Authority

Faith, in its truest form, is not force—it is agreement.

Somewhere along the way, many of us inherited a subtle assumption that faith is the act of *trying harder* to get God to do something. As though intensity were the currency of Heaven. As though repetition were proof. As though volume were power.

But Scripture never presents faith as striving to persuade God. **Faith is alignment with what God has already spoken.** Heaven is not moved by panic. Heaven responds to resonance.

When Jesus says, "My sheep hear (receive) My voice," He is not offering an aspiration; He is stating spiritual law. Recognition happens when frequencies match. Agreement precedes authority.

And Here is where your life becomes very honest, very quickly—because faith is never neutral. Whatever your inner life is aligned with, your faith will amplify.

Faith aligned with fear amplifies distortion.
Faith aligned with pride amplifies illusion.
Faith aligned with self amplifies noise.

But faith aligned with God produces clarity, peace, authority, and fruit.

Authority does not come from assertion—it flows from alignment. Heaven entrusts weight only where posture can sustain it. This is why humility sharpens discernment, stillness clarifies perception, and obedience unlocks authority. Faith does not make God speak louder; it makes us hear clearer.

And hearing clearly changes everything. Because when you hear Him rightly, you stop building on sand. You stop reacting to shadows. You stop calling anxiety "wisdom." You stop confusing urgency with obedience. You begin to recognize the quiet, steady strength of a life that is tuned to the Word.

Could it be that faith is less about making something happen… and more about coming into harmony with what is already true?

When Decree Matches Design — Speaking From Truth, Not Desire

Decree is not the declaration of want—it is the echo of truth.

This is where many sincere believers get weary: they have spoken many things, declared many things, hoped many things… yet inside, something has remained unstable. Because decree without alignment becomes strain. It becomes a kind of spiritual noise—words driven by desire, not rooted in design.

When decree flows from desire, it creates noise.
When it flows from alignment, it establishes reality.

Scripture is clear that what is spoken in agreement with God's will carries weight because it originates in Him. Not in ego. Not in panic. Not in the need to control outcomes. But in the steady authority of the One who sees the end from the beginning.

The believer does not command God. The believer echoes God.

And that is not weakness—it is a holy kind of strength. Because when you echo God, you are not trying to generate power; you are cooperating with it. You are not pretending to be sovereign; you are aligning with sovereignty.

This is why God guards His power through posture. Power divorced from humility corrupts. Revelation without submission inflates. Knowledge without obedience fractures into pride. But when decree matches divine design, it becomes creative rather than consumptive.

Authority is never seized. It is inherited.

And inheritance has a tone. It sounds like sonship and daughterhood. It speaks from belonging, not striving. It is calm enough to wait, confident enough to obey, joyful enough to worship before the evidence arrives.

If your words have felt thin lately, perhaps Heaven is not punishing you. Perhaps you are being invited to return to alignment—so that what you speak is not a coping mechanism, but a partnership.

The Whole Is Greater Than the Part — Corporate Resonance

No single revelation contains the fullness of God.

Even the most breathtaking encounter is still only a facet of infinite light. Even the clearest word you have received is still a portion. Scripture reminds us that we see in part—not because God withholds, but because formation requires humility. Partial knowledge invites dependence. Corporate resonance completes what individual insight cannot.

And perhaps this is one of the hidden protections of God: He refuses to let you become your own source.

The Sound of God was never meant to be hosted in isolation. Harmony requires more than one note. The Body of Christ resonates most clearly when individual lives are tuned to the same Source.

Submission does not diminish revelation—it enlarges it.

This is not the kind of submission that silences your voice or suppresses the Spirit's work in you. It is the kind that recognizes you are part of something holy and whole. It is the humility that says, "I will not make my partial sight into a full doctrine. I will not build a kingdom around my own perspective. I will stay teachable, rooted, and joined."

And when you do—something happens that is difficult to replicate alone: your discernment strengthens, your humility deepens, your love matures. You begin to recognize God not only in your private stillness, but in the shared resonance of worship, community, accountability, and the lived wisdom of the saints.

Could it be that God often confirms His voice through the peace and harmony He produces among His people—when the same Word is ringing in more than one heart?

Living as a Settled Sound — Becoming Unshakable in Him

This is where the journey resolves. Not into certainty of information—but into stability of being.

When truth becomes settled, striving ceases. When striving ceases, clarity remains. When clarity remains, faith becomes sustainable. You no longer chase revelation as though God is always a step ahead of you, withholding Himself until you finally get it right. You begin to host what He has already revealed.

Your life becomes a resonant instrument—consistent, faithful, unshaken.

And this is not because life stops being difficult. It is because the foundation stops being negotiable. The storms still come, but they find less to grab onto. The winds still blow, but they cannot rename what God has said. The culture still shifts, but it no longer determines your internal climate.

The Sound of God has never been absent. It has been waiting for resonance.

So let this chapter be a place you return to—not as a checklist, but as a tuning fork. Let it re—center you. Let it remind you. Let it restore the simplicity of faith: agreement with God.

And let it lead you into declaration—not declaration that tries to control the future, but declaration that seals what is true.

Alignment as Protection

Alignment is not only a way of hearing—it is a way of being kept.

Because there is an enemy of your soul who does not need to silence God in order to derail you. He only needs to distort the signal. He only needs to introduce a believable interference pattern—half-truths wrapped in spiritual language, accusations dressed as conviction, emotional urgency masquerading as wisdom. And if alignment is not practiced as discipline, you will find yourself reacting to impressions that feel spiritual but produce the fruit of separation: anxiety, confusion, self-protection, suspicion, and retreat.

This is why alignment is not optional. It is protection.

The discipline of alignment trains you to distrust what is unstable and cling to what is constant. It teaches you to measure the inner atmosphere by the unchanging Word rather than the weather of your emotions. Emotions can be loud, convincing—even prophetic in tone—yet unreliable in leadership. They are real, but they are not always true. They betray us not by existing, but by becoming our authority.

When emotions become authority, distortion finds an open door. Suddenly the heart interprets God through fear instead of interpreting fear through God.

So you seek first the Kingdom—not as a slogan, but as a survival practice. You discipline yourself toward reverence, stillness, Scripture, and agreement. You stop asking, *What do I feel right now?* as your primary compass, and begin asking, *What has God said, and where am I aligned?* You remember that the Kingdom is steady even when your nervous system is not. You trust what is constant: the nature of God, the character of Christ, the counsel of the Spirit, the reliability of the Word.

And you refuse to give way to guilt, shame, or fear—because these are not neutral emotions; they are weapons. They are the enemy's ancient languages of distortion. Shame whispers that you are disqualified from nearness. Guilt tries to make you repay what Christ has already carried. Fear suggests that God is unsafe, impatient, or disappointed. All three share the same goal: separation. Not always from belief—but from confidence. Not always from Scripture—but from access. Not always from the idea of God—but from the felt permission to draw near.

But the gospel gives you a different reflex. It teaches you that your moment of need is not the moment to shrink back—it is the moment to come closer.

Scripture does not romanticize our weakness, yet it refuses to let weakness become a wall. *"Let us then with confidence draw near to the throne of grace, that we may receive mercy and find grace to help in time of need"* (Hebrews 4:16). Notice what this reveals: there will be times of need—moments when you feel exposed, tempted, confused, burdened, or weary. The instruction is not to hide until you are stable. The instruction is shockingly intimate—draw near with confidence. Need is not disqualifying; it is the very place grace was designed to meet you.

So alignment becomes your practiced response to accusation. When the enemy whispers, *Back away,* alignment answers, *I will draw near.* When shame says, *God does not want you close,* alignment replies, *The throne is not a courtroom for the redeemed—it is a throne of grace.* When fear insists, *You must fix yourself first,* alignment answers, *Mercy meets me now, and help is given in the moment I need it.*

This is the discipline—not clenched intensity, but steady return. A repeated choosing. A holy retraining of instinct. You learn to interpret your emotions in the presence of God rather than interpret God through your emotions. You treat guilt, shame, and fear as alarms—signals that something is pulling you out of resonance—not as voices to obey.

Little by little, your soul becomes guarded—not by isolation, but by intimacy; not by control, but by alignment; not by perfect days, but by confident approach. It is at the Throne of Grace—close enough to receive mercy, steady enough to be helped, and aligned enough to hear the Sound of God even when the enemy tries to counterfeit the frequency.

What began as a question has become an unveiling. Faith was never meant to fear truth, because truth has always belonged to God. The deeper we listen, the more creation itself bears witness: beneath the noise, beneath the arguments, beneath the fractured language of religion and reason, there remains an unbroken reality—God still speaks. His voice is not in competition with the world He made, but revealed through it, above it, and beyond it. And if that is true, then faith is not a blind leap into darkness, but a response to the resonance of what has been true all along. The invitation of this book is not merely to admire that possibility, but to live awake to it.

So let this be your axiom: God is not absent, silent, or unknowable. He is speaking, sustaining, revealing, and drawing near. The question is no longer whether He can be found, but whether we are willing to become still enough, honest enough, and aligned enough to hear Him.

This is where the journey of these pages must become your own. Not in theory alone, but in practice. Not in borrowed language, but in living revelation.

The signal remains. The Word still resounds.

And those willing to seek Him will discover that the sound they have been searching for was never leading them away from truth, but deeper into the heart of it.

The Axioms of Faith & Decree

A Quick Reference for Alignment

Axiom	Law Type (Physics Parallel)	Spiritual Principle	Observable Spiritual Effect	Scriptural Anchor
I. Alignment Produces Likeness	Resonance Law	What is aligned with God reflects God	Character, fruit, and outcomes mirror His nature	Amos 3:3
II. The Word Amplifies Faith	Constructive Interference	Faith strengthened by Scripture gains authority	Clarity, confidence, spiritual power	Romans 10:17
III. Separation Produces Distortion	Signal Attenuation	Removing God diminishes clarity	Confusion, pride, false wisdom	John 15:5
IV. Resonance Enables Recognition	Frequency Matching	God's voice is recognized by those who carry His frequency	Discernment, intimacy, guidance	John 10:27
V. The Whole Exceeds the Part	Systems Theory	God's design surpasses partial understanding	Humility, trust, maturity	1 Cor. 13:9–12
VI. Stillness Sharpens Reception	Noise Reduction Principle	Quiet hearts receive clearer signals	Revelation, peace, stability	Psalm 46:10
VII. Aligned Decree Establishes Reality	Wave Projection / Field Effect	Decree spoken carries Heaven's weight	Authority, establishment, fruitfulness	Job 22:28

A Prayer of Agreement. *(Encouraged to be read aloud)*

Creator God (Elohim), I come to You with reverence and relief—because You are not changing, You are not confused, and You are not far away. You are faithful and true, the same yesterday, today, and forever. Your consistency is not coldness—it is kindness. It is love I can lean on.

I acknowledge that You are present and speaking. Not distant. Not silent. You are near, revealing Yourself to those who make room for you and still themselves to receive from Your voice.

I choose agreement over striving.
I choose alignment over effort.
I choose truth over noise.

I quiet my heart before You and release the pace that has kept me restless. I lay down the need to control outcomes and the habit of listening to my own thoughts louder than Your Word.

Lord, tune me.

I submit my understanding to Your wisdom. Forgive the ways I have tried to secure myself apart from You—through performance, overthinking, and spiritual noise. Thank You that clarity is not something I must manufacture, but something You freely give.

I align my faith with Your Word.
I align my voice with Your design.
I align my life with Your purpose.

I declare that Your Word is true—whether I feel it or not.
I declare that Your voice is faithful—whether circumstances agree or not.
I declare that I belong to You, and that belonging is the beginning of discernment.

Father, let my spirit be tuned to Your Sound. Renew my mind by Your truth. Make my ***Heart*** *a holy habitation of Your presence and let my life resonate with what You have spoken. Seal this journey in me—not as information gained, but as alignment received. Let what You have revealed shape my choices, sanctify my desires, and steady me when the world shakes.*

And when I speak, let my words be an echo—not of fear or striving, but of Heaven. Teach me to listen before I lead, and to agree before I act.

Thank You for Your patience, Your nearness, and the kindness of Your voice. I receive Your invitation with gratitude, respond with commitment, and rejoice in Your faithfulness.

For the joy of knowing You as You truly are, and for Your glory alone.

Amen.

Final Thoughts…

Every journey eventually arrives at a point of clarity.

Not because every question has been answered,
but because the right question has been revealed.

If there is one truth to carry forward from these pages, it is this:

God is not silent.

The patterns woven through creation, the order within sound, and the testimony of Scripture all point toward the same reality—there is a Voice, and it has been speaking all along.

The wandering was never evidence of absence.
It was an invitation to seek more deeply.

And now, having reached this point, the question is no longer whether God can be known.

It is whether you will begin to recognize Him.

Not only in what you read, but in what you observe…
what you discern… and what you choose to align with moving forward.

This is the resolution of the journey:

That faith is not the abandonment of reason, but the alignment of it. That God is not in conflict with truth but revealed through it.

And that what once felt distant or uncertain may have been present and consistent all along.

You have not reached the end of understanding. But you have arrived at something foundational— a place from which to see differently, to listen more carefully, and to move forward with clarity. And you do not have to explore them alone.

Because what has been set in motion here is not confined to these pages. It continues—in the questions you carry, the conversations you engage, and the awareness you choose to cultivate moving forward.

And perhaps this is where it truly begins— not in having all the answers, but in learning to recognize the Voice that has been speaking all along. He is always reaching for you. And you have always been designed to hear Him.

This is the Sound of God.

Join the Conversation…

It was never meant to be an end of the exploration for you — only the beginning. If this book resonated with you, you're not alone.

Join the conversation, access additional resources and explore your faith journey with like-minded community at:

Website: **remnantrising.online**
Instagram: **remant.rising.co**
Facebook: **Remnant Rising Co**

About the Author….

Marcia Alverson is a seasoned author, worship leader, and speaker on worship and spiritual formation. In her 30 + years of ministry, it has been her JOY to build God's kingdom alongside others and help shape several ministries in worship and discipleship across the globe.

With a bachelor's in music education and Master's in Practical Theology, she has spent a majority of her lifetime developing training programs and writing curriculum and songs - providing resources and equipping the local church and the Body of Christ at large.

She has personally taught and mentored thousands of believers in the area of worship & music ministry. Her greatest discovery is that surrendering to God's voice leads to some pretty awesome adventures and is by far the most fulfilling purpose under the sun.

End Notes

Cymatics is the study of the visualization of sound and vibration, often demonstrated by placing particles on vibrating surfaces. The modern field was pioneered by Hans Jenny in the 20th century in his work *Cymatics: A Study of Wave Phenomena and Vibration.* Basel: Macromedia Publishing, 1967–1974.

Resonance and frequency matching: In physics, resonance occurs when a system vibrates at greater amplitude when exposed to a frequency matching its natural frequency. See Richard Feynman, *The Feynman Lectures on Physics*, Vol. 1 (Oscillations and Resonance).

Faith as frequency, not argument: A poetic reframing of faith as relational resonance rather than rational persuasion. Not a scientific claim, but a theological metaphor.

Creation bearing the signature of speech: order, pattern, rhythm, resonance: This blends theological assertions with scientific metaphors. Rooted in the biblical idea of creation through the spoken Word (e.g., Genesis 1, John 1).

Stillness is not emptiness; it is tuning: This metaphor suggests alignment and receptivity as spiritual practices. While borrowing from signal theory language, it is used allegorically.

Entrainment and synchronization: The tendency of oscillating systems to synchronize was first documented by Christiaan Huygens in 1665 when he observed two pendulum clocks gradually aligning their motion when mounted on the same structure.

Nigel Stanford's music video of cymatics & educational experiments: (the video that started the author's exploration of cymatics & faith) https://youtu.be/Q3oItpVa9fs?si=QwkaS71xLrC5v23V

Sound waves as energy/information shaping reality: In physics, sound travels as mechanical pressure waves that transmit energy and can affect matter. This paragraph builds a bridge between physical science and spiritual implication.

Logos (Word) as creative principle: The concept of divine speech as creative order appears in both biblical theology (Genesis 1; John 1:1–3) and classical philosophical discussions of the Logos, particularly in early Christian writings engaging Greek philosophical traditions.

Quote often attributed to Nikolai Tesla: "If you want to find the secrets of the universe, think in terms of energy, frequency, and vibration" Widely quoted online but not verified in Tesla's documented writings.

"Word" and "breath" as metaphors for physical resonance: This interpretation weaves biblical terms with physics language. Intended as a metaphor, not a doctrinal or empirical assertion.

Other works and scientific papers for reference:

Hunt, Julian. *The Universe Within: A Scientific Adventure.*

Gleick, James. *Chaos: Making a New Science.*

Frequency organizes matter into ordered patterns: "Chladni Plate and Chladni Patterns — A Research Review of Theory, Modelling, Simulation and Engineering Applications."

A study of self-organization and wave dynamics in modern physics research: "Point-Driven Modern Chladni Figures with Symmetry Breaking." *Scientific Reports (Nature Publishing).*

Alignment and resonance between systems: "Huygens' Synchronization Experiment Revisited."

Experimental Cymatics Modal Analysis: "Modal Analysis of Chladni Plate Using Cymatics."

Sound-Generated Geometric Patterns: "Effects of Geometric Sound on Brainwave Activity Patterns."

Author's Clarification

While this book draws thoughtful parallels between scientific observations—particularly in the study of sound, resonance, and frequency—and spiritual truths found in Scripture, it is not intended to claim that the voice of God can be measured or scientifically verified through these phenomena.

Rather, these references are offered to illuminate meaningful parallels between the natural world and the spiritual realities described in the Holy Bible. Throughout history, creation itself has served as a witness to deeper truths about its Creator. Artistry gives us a glimpse of the world through the eyes of the Artist.

And perhaps that matters because we, too, are works of art—formed with intention, beauty, and purpose. The "He-art" design is significant. The Heart is not merely a biological center; it is a central hub of spirit, soul, and body, where affection, perception, surrender, and life itself begin and return. It is God's signature within His most intimate artwork: humanity.

According to the perspective of this author, the realm of faith is where these reflections converge—where the observable world and the unseen work of God invite deeper exploration. In that space, faith becomes not merely belief, but the substance that guides our journey toward Truth and reveals our place in his Grand Design.

www.ingramcontent.com/pod-product-compliance
Lightning Source LLC
LaVergne TN
LVHW090521110826
845146LV00003B/940

* 9 7 9 8 9 9 5 4 3 5 7 0 9 *